You Only Live Once

You Only Live Once

The Roadmap to Financial
Wellness and a Purposeful Life

Jason Vitug

WILEY

Published by John Wiley & Sons, Inc., Hoboken, New Jersey.
Published simultaneously in Canada.

Library of Congress Cataloging-in-Publication Data:
Names: Vitug, Jason, author.
Title: You only live once : the roadmap to financial wellness and a
    purposeful life / Jason Vitug.
Description: Hoboken : Wiley, 2016. | Includes index.
Identifiers: LCCN 2016010707 (print) | LCCN 2016011195 (ebook) |
ISBN 978-1-119-26736-2 (hardback) | ISBN 978-1-119-26737-9 (epdf) |
ISBN 978-1-119-26742-3 (epub)
Subjects: LCSH: Finance, Personal. | BISAC: BUSINESS & ECONOMICS / Personal
    Finance / Budgeting.
Classification: LCC HG179 .V588 2016 (print) | LCC HG179 (ebook) | DDC
    332.024—dc23
LC record available at http://lccn.loc.gov/2016010707

Printed in the United States of America

10 9 8 7 6 5 4 3 2 1

I am the product of your hopes and dreams.

I dedicate this book to my parents. Thank you for being such an inspiration to me. Your absolute love and support through the years have made me into the man I am today. You have taught me the valuable lessons of focus, compassion, and humility. I am fortunate to have you as parents in this lifetime. I love you both very much.

Contents

Preface   ix

Acknowledgments   xv

About the Author   xix

Introduction   1

Part I   On the Road to Financial Wellness **5**

Chapter 1   Are You Living YOLO?   7
The Millennial Experience   7
The YOLO Mindset   8

Chapter 2   Financial Education and Living Your
              Dream Lifestyle   11
What Is Financial Education?   13
The ACT Process   14

Part II   Awareness **15**

Chapter 3   Know Where You're Starting From   17
Your Money Mindset   18
What Is Your Relationship with Money?   19
How Is Your Spending Contributing to Your Life?   20
How Are You Using Your Time?   22
Cultivate a Wealthy Money Mindset   23

Chapter 4   Know Where You Want to Go   31
Clarify Your Values   32
Have a Vision for Your Life   35
Follow a Money Philosophy   38

Chapter 5   Getting What You Want   41
Change Your Financial Behaviors and Habits   41
The Habit of Spending   42
The Habit of Saving   43
Get in the Know   45

Part III   Creating a Plan **63**

   Chapter 6   Building a Lifestyle Budget and Spending Plan   67
     Dealing with Your Fear of Lifestyle Change   70
     Living the YOLO Lifestyle   74
     The YOLO Budget   77

   Chapter 7   Using the Purposeful Money Strategy to Spend
            and Save   97
     Dual Checking Accounts Method   98
     The Purposeful Savings Method   101

   Chapter 8   Improving Credit Use and Eliminating
            Debt Forever   111
     Credit Card Debt   115
     Using the Debt Avalanche Method   117
     Using the Debt Snowball Method   118

Part IV   Taking Control **121**

   Chapter 9   Creating a Purposeful Life   123
     Finding Happiness   124
     Increasing Your Awareness   126
     Organizing Your Finances   128
     Managing Your Time   130
     Having Better Conversations   132
     Improving Financial Relationships   134

   Chapter 10   Spending Rules   137
     Spending Mindfully   138
     Spend Less Than You Earn   139
     Pay Less for Every Purchase   139
     Spend on Loves, Not Likes   140
     Use Credit Purposefully   142

   Chapter 11   Living Mindfully   145
     Building Your Freedom Fund   146
     Don't Quit Your Job   148
     Traveling the World   151
     Lending Money to Family and Friends   152
     Making Money with Money: Investing   153
     Protecting Your Legacy: Insurance   155
     Finding an Expert   156

   Conclusion   159

   Index   161

Preface

Years ago I remember seeing an old Army recruiting commercial that asked the question, "If someone wrote a story about your life, would anyone want to read it?" The question wasn't profound because it made me want to join the military; rather, it made me question the life I was then living. I was at a crossroads, wondering what happened to my dreams.

I grew up in Elizabeth—the fourth-largest city in New Jersey—raised by two amazing, hardworking immigrant parents. I was one of five children, the second youngest and the middle boy. I had lived in seven different houses by the time I entered high school. My parents stretched their dollars to provide for a family of seven. My parents didn't talk about money, but I also never worried about shelter, food, or my health. They made sure those needs were met. I didn't grow up with brand-name labels, and our idea of fine dining was eating at buffet restaurants. We walked around the mall to stretch our legs, but most of my clothes were hand-me-downs from my older brother.

I was the dreamer and the overachiever who got good grades and followed the rules. As a teenager I made money by delivering pizza, mowing lawns, raking leaves, and shoveling snow. I competed in forensics, played sports, and acted in school plays. I was class president and a member of the honor society. I also graduated at the top of my class.

I had a dream for my life and I was eager to start college.

During my senior year of high school, my mother told me that they couldn't pay my college tuition. It was the first conversation about money that I had ever had. Although on paper my parents' income was over the limit for me to be eligible for financial aid, their actual disposable income wasn't enough to afford to send me to school.

I was devastated.

Without enough money for college, it meant I wasn't going anywhere after high school. I was ashamed. I didn't even tell my friends. I quietly got a job at Newark Airport instead.

I deferred going to college for a year and worked long hours to save as much as I could to afford the first year's tuition. The following fall I was able to enroll at school full time but continued to work at the airport. I did well at work and was promoted. I made good money. After four years I graduated with a bachelor's degree in finance but with a mountain of debt from my student loans and credit cards.

I never attended a financial-education class in high school or college. I was taught how to calculate the area of a triangle but not the power of compounding interest. I learned the periodic table of elements but not how the banking system operates. I had classes in the arts, music, and physical education, but the important lessons that can impact our ability to have our dream careers—as artists, musicians, and athletes—weren't offered in the classroom.

I wasn't prepared to make any financial decisions.

My first experience with a credit card began in college. I was hanging with friends at the common area when I was approached by someone who looked like a student, who asked if I wanted a Frisbee. I only had to do one thing: Complete an application.

I wanted a Frisbee. So I quickly completed and signed the application. A few weeks later, a plastic card of financial opportunities arrived.

My parents used credit cards. I marveled at their designs and was awed by how easily a purchase could be made. I saw my parents pay for groceries, clothing, and essentials with a single swipe. I wondered who gave them free money. I wondered who would give me free money. I imagined that this plastic card would empower me to get anything I wanted. And now, I had my own.

My first credit card had a credit limit of $500. I was responsible for making the small and affordable minimum monthly payments on time, every time. I was rewarded for my money-management skills with a higher credit limit. But my outstanding balance increased accordingly. I never thought of the total balance owed, because the minimum payments were paid. By the time I graduated college, the $500-limit credit card had turned into a $5,000 balance. I cannot recall what I spent with the $5,000, but I do remember the Frisbee.

This is how I bought a $5,000 Frisbee.

After college, I didn't find myself living my dreams. I was barely living. I just existed to pay off student loans and credit card debt. I found myself working a number of jobs that weren't at all satisfying. I found myself further and further away from the life I'd envisioned as a teenager. My days weren't filled with excitement and world-changing work. They were filled with endless consumption, debt, and enough what-if statements to fill a book of their own.

I got a job in banking and progressed in a career, and my salary grew along with it. I went from working a job cleaning toilets and serving drinks to one as an executive who made decisions in the boardroom seven and a half years later. I lived in an apartment in Silicon Valley with a walk-in closet that was the size of a room I once shared with my two brothers. I owned two cars, a bike, a closet filled with clothes, and shelves of unused gadgets. I appeared to be the model of success, but underneath it was a much different story.

I was professionally successful but personally unsatisfied. I was income-stable but financially inept. I was the poster child for bad financial decision making. I paid hundreds of dollars in overdraft penalties and fees for nonsufficient funds. I racked up tens of thousands of dollars in credit card debt. I had student loans. I consolidated and reconsolidated unsecured credit. I took out loans from my 401(k). I used IRA money to pay for monthly expenses. Even on a six-figure salary, I lived paycheck-to-paycheck.

I was dissatisfied. I was unhappy. I was out of control.

Money was the obstacle to my dreams. I came from a place of fear and scarcity. I chased money as the solution to my problems and believed my ability to spend corresponded with control. After one financial mistake and more bad decisions, I no longer dreamed of a better life. I had become indebted to something I had mindlessly created.

I needed a change.

I immersed myself in financial education. I learned how to budget and pay off debt. I paid off over $40,000 in unsecured debt and $15,000 in student loans. I learned how to save money and invest for my retirement. I felt on the top of my game. I was free of consumer debt. I had an emergency fund, as well as vacation and holiday club savings. I was contributing to my 401(k) and Roth IRAs. I was investing through my company's employee stock purchase program and buying stocks through my brokerage accounts.

I had achieved financial success and set financial goals, but without a sense of purpose I returned to my old ways—mindlessly consuming and obsessively complaining.

All the how-to seminars, blogs, books, and apps helped me to achieve goals, but they didn't go far enough. They didn't help me to uncover the real why behind my desire for financial freedom. It no longer mattered that I was debt free or that my savings had increased exponentially. I had reached a point at which I was yearning for something different. I had all this financial knowledge, but I didn't know how to apply it to living a purposeful life.

Society told me I was successful, but my doctor told me I was stressed. After three years as a successful executive, I became determined to gain this financial freedom. I declined job offers that came with a larger salary. And instead of pursuing the path to succeed the CEO, I resigned.

In January 2012, I made a decision that started a journey that altered the trajectory of my life. For as long as I could remember, I had followed a specific path that society states is the way to happiness and success: graduate high school, make money, finish college, get a job, buy a car, get promoted, own a home—and somewhere in between, find the love of my life, start a family, and begin planning for retirement. Even though I went off track sometimes, I forced myself back on this path.

Eventually I realized that I wasn't getting any happier, but instead growing more and more dissatisfied. I had no control over my life, and my financial situation mimicked that lack of control. I began asking others about happiness and was repeatedly told to continue on the path.

"You seem entitled," they said.

They wanted me to accept that if I just continued as I was, I could retire in my 70s and become happy after that. I refused to accept the idea that I needed to work 45 more years to (hopefully) live the dreams I once had as a teenager.

I sold or donated everything I owned and paid off what I owed. I stopped spending and setting up financial goals. I began prioritizing life goals.

I left my executive job to find my way. That step led to a backpacking trip around the world through 20 countries in 12 months, during which I explored Southeast Asia, Central America, and Western Europe. I had new conversations that gave me new insights. I discovered new interests and learned to define my purpose. I came home with a vision for my life.

How was it that someone like me was able to take a different path?

I learned that knowledge is power, but financial knowledge is life changing. My past experiences had shaped my relationship with money, creating an unhealthy money mindset that clouded my mind and limited my ability to do the things I wanted to. My awareness and acceptance of this relationship allowed me to shift my mindset and change my financial habits. This has enabled me to live my dream lifestyle in *this* lifetime.

I am satisfied. I am happy. I am in control.

In the course of my studies, research, and conversations around the world and during my epic road trip—the Road to Financial Wellness— I learned that we need to evaluate our relationship with money and increase our financial intelligence in order to make better financial decisions and shape our dream lifestyle. By confronting my scarcity mindset and addressing my fears about money, I realized the power of having a vision for my life and setting financial goals that align with my values.

I am living my purpose, and in the pages of this book I hope to educate and inspire you to take the next steps to improve your relationship with money so that you, too, can live your dream lifestyle in this lifetime.

Acknowledgments

This book is based on years of experience and is influenced by the many amazing people who have contributed to my life's story. I hold you dear in my heart and am appreciative of the love you've given me throughout the years.

This book would not have been possible without three amazing people who believed in my message and connected me to my publisher, John Wiley & Sons. Many thanks go to Marge and George Alexander and to Fred Wied IV. I also thank my Wiley team: Tula Batanchiev, associate editor, who after hearing my story and idea for the book, cheered me on; and Kathryn Duggan, my development editor, who took my ramblings and helped develop the story and flow.

To the thousands of people I met on the Road to Financial Wellness tour, I thank you for listening to my story and sharing yours. And to the Phroogal community and those living the Smile Lifestyle: This book was inspired by you.

To my road trip team: Larry Valente Solha, Austin Strickland, Juliana Anselmini, Melanie Lockert, and Will Lipovsky, who made the Road to Financial Wellness tour a success. I couldn't have done this without you.

To Yaroslav Tashak, who after hearing my story during a Montclair State University entrepreneurship event offered his help in making my dream come true. Thank you for joining me on the road trip and spending an additional 14 days to head back home. Your friendship has been influential and invaluable to me.

There were 47 personal finance bloggers, podcasters, financial educators, and presenters who supported the road trip, and I wish I could list all of you here. Thank you for spreading the word to your communities. I am grateful to each and every one of you.

A very special thanks to Carey Ransom and the team at Payoff for their national sponsorship of the Road to Financial Wellness—they made it possible for my team to trek across the country for 30 days in order to break the social taboo of talking about money.

Thank you to the National Credit Union Foundation, aSmarterChoice .org, the World Council of Credit Unions, and the credit unions that believed in my vision: Denver Community Credit Union, Combined Employees Credit Union, 121 Financial Credit Union, Midwest Community Federal Credit Union, ISU Credit Union, Aspire Federal Credit Union, Lake Trust Credit Union, Camino Federal Credit Union, Affinity Federal Credit Union, Missoula Federal Credit Union, Parkside Credit Union, Horizon Credit Union, Ravalli County Federal Credit Union, and Donya Parrish of Montana Credit Union Network.

A special thanks to Mark Cochran of Jeanne D'Arc Credit Union, Michele Bolkovatz of Warren Federal Credit Union, and Fadhila Holman of Cooperative Center Federal Credit Union—the first three people who jumped at the chance to be part of the nationwide financial wellness campaign.

To the nonprofits that supported our mission across the country— mPowered of Colorado, Inceptia, Creative Portland, Junior Achievement of New York, Greater Newark Enterprise Corporation, Urban League of Union County Young Professionals, Someone's Daughter, Consumers United Association of Colorado, Equality Washington, New Community Church, and Columbia North YMCA—I thank you.

Thanks also to Republic Wireless, Experian, Wisebread, MoneyCrashers, XY Planning Network, Quizzle, Shim's Martial Arts Academy, Galvanize Denver, Opodz, Simple Bank, SoFi, Vincent Turner of SF FinTech meetup, and Carlos Abad of LaunchNJ for opening your communities to our message.

And thank you to the Denver Office of Strategic Partnerships and to my hometown mayor, the Honorable J. Christian Bollwage of Elizabeth, New Jersey.

I also extend my gratitude to Barbara O'Neill of Rutgers University Cooperative Extension, Nicole Didomenico of Norwich University, Sharon Waters of the Feliciano Center for Entrepreneurship, and Carmen Cuevas of Montclair State University for giving me the opportunity to educate students about money and purpose.

I owe so much to Philip Taylor, the founder of FinCon, who in 2013 gave me a free ticket to attend his conference in St. Louis, which helped me to build my network and exposed me to an amazing community, and to J. Money, of BudgetsAreSexy.com, for his time and mentorship.

I was also successful because of on-the-road support from Joe Saul-Sehy of Stacking Benjamins, Tiffany "the Budgetnista" Aliche, Patrice "the Money Maven" Washington, Tarra Jackson of Ms. Madam Money, and Farnoosh Torabi—to all of you, much appreciation for sharing your tips and supporting my cause; to Steve Stewart, who coached me on giving better podcast interviews; and to Austin Netzley for my very first podcast interview.

For setting up events, I am beholden to Ralph Carmona, Sandy Smith, Dave Olverson, Kate Dore, Leslie Girone, Chenell Tull, Alan Steinborn, Adam Muller, Alyssa Windell, Abdul Taylor, Eva Baker, Katie Brewer, Deacon Hayes, Athena Lent, Miranda Marquit, Talaat and Tai McNeely of HisandHerMoney.com, and Zach the Froogal Stoodent. I am also beholden to Steve and Annette Economides of MoneySmartFamily.com for opening up your home, Michelle Jackson for rounding up bloggers in Denver, Leisa Peterson of WealthClinic, Aaron Goodnow and William Cristobal of Yoga Belly Studio, Bill Dwight of FamZoo for making sure we ate healthy on the road, and Kate Blanchard and Jeff Fruhwirth for introducing me to credit union sponsors.

Many thanks to my teachers: Jeffrey Schneider, who coached me on the forensics team, to which I attribute my success as a speaker; and Anthony Nufrio, my drama teacher, who gave me the opportunity to shine on stage.

I was also given many opportunities to grow professionally thanks to Tricia Kearney-Casalinho, Ana Fernades-Moreira, Anabela Fonseca, and Emini Gidi, who challenged me in my first job at Newark Airport; Mark Charbonneau and Caterine Dobrzanski, who hired me at age 22 and gave me my first banking job; Marcia Waithe, who taught me everything she knew; Mary Sciaraffo and Ellen McGuinness-Ford, who gave me opportunities to grow; Donna LoStocco, who said I had "compassionate determination"; and my dearest friend Nicole Goodspeed—who took me under her wing and said, "One day I'll be reporting to you"—you are forever in my heart, I miss you.

My life wouldn't be where it is today without the opportunity that was given to me by Christine Petro, who became my boss, mentor, and friend. Thank you for believing in this passionate yet unpolished "kid." Tony Ward-Smith, thank you for your guidance, which helped me to make the tough decision to leave my career and take a chance.

Thanks to my human resources friends who helped start me on this road and are still a part of my life: Cristina Valverde and her efforts to make me part of the TE Menlo Park campus; Linda Grant, who gave the initial recommendation that changed the trajectory of my career; and Darlene Lehman, who managed to fill every seat for every one of my workplace financial literacy seminars.

To some amazing friends—I am honored by your continued friendship specifically during this time, and I thank you for lending your ears through the years: Leonardo Cortes, Jessica Luciano, Oscar Alfaro, Hugo Esteves, Chihui Seo, Renato Carniero, Tony Masia, Ralph Bijasa, Eddie Morais, Ana Dias, Michael Matvienko, Kyle Taylor, Paul Fidalgo, Justin Heaton, and Kelly Hrycenko. Thanks also to Galen Schultz and Michelle Phan, who opened their home to my team in Raleigh; Melba Fidalgo, who offered me my first opportunity to share my story, at Playworks in Newark, New Jersey; Meg Fry for my first newspaper editorial; and Gavin Vallance, Albert Garcia, Chris Fernandes, and Javier Ponce, who helped me through difficult moments in my life. I thank you all.

Thank you to Max Martinez, who believed in my vision for Phroogal and helped me to successfully crowd-fund my passion project, and to the 541 people who contributed to the campaign. I am forever grateful. Thank you to my aunts and uncles who let me crash on their couches and financially supported my goals during this period: Edel and Conrado Bautista and Gil and Jo Ramos.

Love to my wonderful and large family: Jennifer, Jeffrey, Janice, and John; to my in-laws, Francisco, Kseniia, David, and Karla; and especially to my 13 nieces and nephews, who I hope will read this book and not make the mistakes I've made: Alexander, Nicolas, Keanu, and Keira; Sophia and Amelia; Adriana, Elena, and Kayla; Greta and the twins, Matilda and Clementine; and my adopted nephew Sebastian.

About the Author

Jason Vitug is an author, speaker, and social impact entrepreneur as founder of personal finance website and lifestyle brand – Phroogal. He is a financial motivator and lifestyle engineer.

Jason is the promoter of The Smile Lifestyle movement, a community of thousands of millennials who are living purposeful lives and making informed financial decisions to stop wasting time and money, and focus on the things that matter. The movement is based on a belief that experiential and purposeful living can be achieved through sound financial decision making.

Jason worked in the financial services industry for almost 8 years and was the Vice President of Marketing and Business Development for a Silicon Valley based credit union that experienced trans-formative growth during his tenure.

In 2012, Jason left his senior executive role and backpacked around the world visiting 20 countries in 12 months. It was in this journey he created his purpose and in 2013 started Phroogal and successfully crowd funded raising $78,501 with the support of 541 people.

Jason is the creator of the award winning project – The Road to Financial Wellness – a grassroots and social media campaign to break the social taboo about money and empower a generation to live their dreams.

Jason grew up in Elizabeth, NJ and attended the Elizabeth Public School system from K-12. He is a graduate of Norwich University and Rutgers University receiving a B.S. in Finance and holds a Masters of Business Administration.

Introduction

This is a book on personal finance. However, it's not a financial-education book or a how-to manual for managing your finances. It is a personal development book to ignite your interest in personal finance, empower you to have a vision for your life, and encourage you to set the right goals to live a rich and purposeful life.

The most powerful reason to increase your financial understanding is to make better financial decisions. There are hundreds of great personal finance books that provide step-by-step instructions on how to budget, save money, pay off debt, and plan for retirement. Although I will be providing budgeting steps and answers to many personal finance questions that you might have, you may find that this book actually challenges your emotions more than your finances. And I do believe that if you continue reading, you will have a better understanding of yourself and will gain an increased awareness of what is most important to you.

I've spent a great deal of time traveling across the country and speaking with thousands of people from all walks of life who have all kinds of financial situations. I'm usually asked for specific advice that will improve a person's finances or provide that one critical answer to address his or her current financial dilemma.

But here is a simple truth. Managing your finances responsibly can be summed up with the following advice: Save more than you spend, invest early and frequently, pay off debt and use credit sparingly, build assets, and create passive income. These simple guidelines have been restated over and over, yet many still are unable to apply these financial principles to their lives. I was one of these people, and you may be too.

Most (if not all) people are seeking a specific plan or the one guideline they need to follow to manage their finances successfully. Sure, I could write an entire book about a specific plan that I believe you need to follow. However, my experience has taught me that all the time spent on providing plans and how-to guides does little to change behaviors. Our behaviors and spending habits are shaped by our money mindsets—how we feel about money. Oftentimes this feeling or relationship that we have with money leads to irrational financial decision making that confounds all rational thinking.

This is why I am sharing my story. It's through stories that we can regain hope. Hope, I once heard during a difficult time in my life, stands for "hearing other people's stories." It was through the stories I heard that I learned my life could change and I could regain control over its direction. So this book is not your run-of-the-mill personal finance book. I've written this book to educate and inspire you to have open conversations about your finances—to break the social taboo of talking about money—and to motivate you to continue your education and apply the knowledge gained toward achieving your goals and living your purpose.

With that said, traditional financial education has its place. Financial education improves your ability to make better decisions today that will help you achieve more of your life goals. When you're making better financial decisions because you have a gained a better understanding of personal finances, you'll find yourself prioritizing advancing your career over making trivial purchases, you'll choose better financial services companies, and you'll find yourself living your dream lifestyle sooner rather than later.

It may seem as if the topics I discuss in this book and the questions I ask of you belong in a personal development book. That is by design. I've written this book with the purpose of helping you uncover those forgotten childhood dreams that weren't dependent on dollars and cents but now have become increasingly unattainable because of your money mindset. Your money mindset is how you think and feel about money, and it creates your money philosophy—a set of guiding principles that you may consciously or unconsciously follow when making financial decisions.

I've read many books, attended many seminars, and used many apps that offer easier ways to do the *how* but have rarely helped me understand my *why*. Financial education continues to focus on providing us with solutions that will fix the results of our decisions, rather than an effective way of preventing us from making them in the first place.

Your money mindset and money philosophy have more to do with why you've been unable to reach your financial goals or live your dream lifestyle than any lack of financial understanding you may have.

Imagine a scenario in which you go into your doctor's office complaining about stomach pains, and you're offered an antacid tablet. Your problem may be solved temporarily, but it may resurface if you're not addressing what caused the problem in the first place. That has been my biggest issue with many of the personal finance books I've read: They provide steps, solutions, and how-tos without addressing the root of the problem—your relationship with money and your money mindset.

You certainly can learn the how of managing money, given that there are many ways to access financial information online and offline, a plethora of step-by-step instructions, and a growing list of calculators and budgeting apps. But even with all of that readily available information, you'll still be challenged to make the financial decisions that best support the life you actually want to live.

I decided I needed to write this book in order to share what I've learned about living a purposeful and rich life. As you read through the chapters, you'll begin to realize that this book is indeed written in a self-help style. Although I have filled these pages with motivational thoughts, they are not empty phrases—my purpose is to make them memorable enough to motivate you into action. You'll learn a great deal about your money mindset, your financial behaviors, and ways to improve your relationship with money. I will also share why you should practice awareness and how you can create a lifestyle budget, save purposefully, spend consciously, and rethink retirement.

The book is divided into four parts.

Part I: On the Road to Financial Wellness: In this part, you'll learn why your financial journey is your life journey and the importance of financial education in empowering yourself.

The next three parts of the book focus on the ACT process: *awareness*, *creating a plan*, and *taking control*. You'll learn more about your relationship with money and how to cultivate the right money mindset and how to improve your financial behaviors. I developed ACT as a way to help you understand the importance of self-awareness in your journey to living a rich and purposeful life.

Part II: Awareness: The chapters in this part will help you get clarity about where you are and where you want to go. It will guide you in becoming more aware of your spending habits and the power of time.

Part III: Creating a Plan: This part walks you through creating a budget that will be the blueprint for the life you want to live. Retirement isn't just an age but a state of living, and with the right plan you can retire sooner rather than later. Through the process of lifestyle budgeting, you'll learn to identify the financial goals that are right for you and create a purposeful savings strategy that supports your vision for your life.

Part IV: Taking Control: This part provides you with processes to follow to help you take control of your finances and your life. With clarity about your values and a vision for your life, you'll learn effective ways to increase your income and spend more mindfully to live your dreams.

Just based on the fact that you're reading this book, I have no doubt that you're well on your way to figuring out what's most important to you. I encourage you to use this book as a guide to help you reshape your money mindset, define your vision, and achieve your goals.

PART I

On the Road to Financial Wellness

I n the summer of 2015, I went on an epic road trip called the Road to Financial Wellness. The road trip was a grassroots and social media experiment to turn local money discussions into a national conversation on financial well-being. My team and I drove 10,218 miles in 30 days, zigzagging across the country and speaking with over 8,000 people in 38 states during the month of June. Our mission was to break the last social taboo—money—and empower people through stories that would educate and inspire them to learn more about personal finance and to live their dream lifestyles.

I wanted people to understand that financial success—however you choose to define that success—only matters if you've found a balance between money and life. I used the term *financial wellness* to describe that state of living in which your well-being is measured by the quality of your life, not just by wealth.

On the road trip I asked seminar attendees to think of their lives as their very own road-trip adventures. We all have a start and an end point. We may not have any control over where we start, but we decide where we end up. The path you choose, the skills you acquire, and the tools you use can go a long way in making your road trip an enjoyable and rewarding ride.

Imagine yourself planning a trip across the country, with a starting point in New York City and an end point on the West Coast. You set off on your adventure with excitement but soon realize you were ill prepared for the journey: The car you chose wasn't well-maintained, and the roads you took at times were scenic but mostly were uninteresting. You relied on your smartphone for a GPS, not knowing that in some parts of the country the service would be unreliable. You got lost and ran out of gas. You sped down small town roads and got a speeding ticket. You had a flat tire, but you had a spare and the skill to change it. When the engine began to sputter, you found yourself stranded by the roadside, questioning your decision to go on the road trip in the first place. Finally, you arrived. You reached the West Coast with your swimming shorts, surfboard, and suntan lotion, but you found yourself in Seattle, not San Diego.

A road trip has twists and turns and unexpected surprises. Sometimes the path is a straight and wide highway, and other times it's a narrow winding road. Most times you're coasting along, enjoying the scenery. Other times, you're stuck in bumper-to-bumper traffic.

You can easily replace those road-trip terms with money terms to represent your financial journey. You grew up in a household with a particular financial situation, but you had a vision for your own life. You weren't exactly sure how you wanted to live, but you knew the things you wanted to do. You didn't grow up with an understanding of personal finances, but you did learn some useful skills that have helped along the way. But as you navigated to adulthood, things began to change unnoticeably. You thought of things, not dreams. You relied heavily on a job for income until it was gone. You paid more in banking fees than you had in your savings account. When you were facing financial difficulties, you questioned your actions. You once had a vision for your life but are now living a life you can't recognize and are set on a directionless path.

You've made financial mistakes, but rest assured, as long as you're still in the driver's seat, you can change course and choose a more scenic path to enjoy the ride and reach your destination.

Take what you've learned. Gain clarity about your vision of life. Set your destination. Now, hop back in your car with a renewed passion, a better plan, and improved skills that will get you from Seattle to San Diego.

CHAPTER 1

Are You Living YOLO?

I used to hear YOLO more often exclaimed while shopping at the mall or taking shots at the bar.

It didn't matter what part of the country I was in or the generations that made up the group I spoke to. People would laugh when I used the term *YOLO*. What was it about YOLO that elicited that response? Was it coming from a place of youthful and joyful carelessness? Or was it a reaction of nervous laughter?

Mae West was quoted as saying, "You only live once, but if you do it right, once is enough."

I wouldn't have thought that someone born in the late 1890s could capture a millennial motto so perfectly. Maybe it's a mindset of any generation born before the turn of any century. Or maybe it's that the desire to live a purposeful life runs across all generations.

THE MILLENNIAL EXPERIENCE

I am a member of Generation Y and proudly accept the word *millennial* to describe my generation, the first to grow into adulthood in this millennium. My baby-boomer parents worked toward a purposeful life, and I am a product of their hopes and dreams. They taught me the valuable lesson that life was hard, but life had meaning. They raised me to believe that I could accomplish anything, and that I should strive to live my dreams. Holding these beliefs to be true, I grew up with a sense of entitlement—that I was entitled to live a life with meaning.

What has happened outside of our households has influenced my generation's view of the world and our place in it as well. As millennials, we experienced the dot-com crash of the late 1990s and the Great Recession during our formative years of personal and career development. We've lived in a constant state of war and terror for most of our lives. We saw the greed of Wall Street and the material excesses of our parents, who bought larger cars and bigger homes, and used equity to finance uncontrolled spending. Then the stock market crashed and our families were faced with financial hardships because of layoffs, home foreclosures, and reduced retirement savings.

It isn't a surprise that as a result of how we grew up, we adopted the motto *YOLO* (which stands for You Only Live Once) as an expression of the uncertainty of tomorrow. Our motto means that you should seize the moment as it happens without a thought about money. We have used our desire to live a carefree life and our uncertainty about our future as guiding principles in making financial decisions. YOLO explains our irrational spending behavior and our preference for experiences over things.

THE YOLO MINDSET

YOLO has influenced our behaviors around banking, saving, spending, and investing. We don't value banks in the traditional sense; we prefer the experience of convenient apps and personal service to meet our banking needs. We know the importance of saving money, but saving is often delayed in favor of paying off student loans—a debt we took on to pay for education we were told we needed to get our dream jobs—or spending on experiences to make up for all the time spent at work and on our side hustles. The YOLO mindset about saving means you're aware of what you value and willing to invest your time to attain it.

We are a generation that loves to share socially—a result of our parents teaching us to share with others. This has made us more susceptible to peer influence and social-marketing tactics, which has influenced our spending habits. We buy things and experiences we don't want in order to give others the illusion of happy lives on social media. We have become compelled to shop more because of targeted ads that follow us online from retailers who know our habits—spending habits we weren't aware we had.

This mindless and uncontrolled spending means allocating more of your future time to work. I personally don't believe in the notion that we must stop all spending. Spending is a part of living. You're spending on what you need and what you want. However, when you're spending mindlessly, you're not in control. I advocate spending money where it matters, and that means being clear about your values—knowing what matters most to you. If in order to buy things you don't value you must spend more time at work, then how much of your life are you actually living? The YOLO mindset about spending means you're aware of what's important and won't sacrifice a lifetime of happiness for short-term gratification.

Growing up during a period that saw two economic crashes has had a profound impact on how we view investing in the stock market, too. We see investing as risky, but we've also seen how quickly the market can recover. Investing is a great way to cultivate a lifestyle of less work by making money with money. The YOLO mindset can be used to prioritize asset building over salary increases. If you only live once, building assets to generate income is the most effective use of your time.

As an older millennial, the YOLO mindset is ingrained in my psyche, and I, too, have used YOLO as an excuse to make irrational financial decisions, but eventually I learned the true value of living YOLO. As the years have gone by, I've learned that tomorrow is as real as today, and the financial choices we make now have a big impact on the life we live in the future. If we only live once, let's make decisions that support a healthy and financially stress-free lifestyle.

The YOLO mindset is ideal when applied to the understanding that today is the best day to start saving, investing, and spending mindfully in order to live a purposeful life. Living YOLO is awareness that our time is our most valuable asset, and that once it is spent, it cannot be repurchased at any price. Time therefore should be used wisely, so that you're doing more of the things you value and fewer of the things you don't. For example:

Saving. You should be aware of what you value and be willing to invest your time to achieve your goals.

Spending. What you spend money on is a reflection of your values. Spend on things that matter the most to you and add value in your life.

Debt. Debt reserves your future time for work rather than fun. Prioritize debt elimination to gain more time for living.

Investing. Growing your assets decreases your need to exchange your time for income. Make money with money.

Remain mindful of your YOLO mindset and how it's impacting your financial behavior. As you continue reading, you'll gain more awareness and can apply this mindset to creating a vision for your life, gaining clarity about your values, and setting the right financial goals.

CHAPTER 2

Financial Education and Living Your Dream Lifestyle

'm a big fan of financial education. Mastering finances is an important life skill because it has such a drastic impact on how you get to live your life and when you get to live it. The more skilled you are in handling money, the less susceptible you will be to making financial mistakes that can derail your efforts to live the life you want. Financial education can help you manage your money more effectively, leading to saving more, earning more, and spending wisely on things that matter.

During my seminars I ask my audience this question: "Why do we learn how to calculate the area of a triangle but not the power of compounding interest?"

I'd pause, scan the room, and continue by asking: "Why are we taught art, music, and physical fitness, yet the banking and investment industry remains a mystery?"

Many, if not all, in the audience nod their heads in agreement.

I have yet to meet someone who hasn't agreed with me on the importance of financial education. Yet even with that truth, I find very few people who actively engage in financial education. Let me get this out of the way: Money is fun. Spending is exciting. But financial education sounds like a bore. Think about where you get most of your traditional financial education from: banks, financial services companies, government agencies, and nonprofits. None of these institutions scream *fun and exciting*.

Without the right financial tools and personal finance skills, you might find that navigating toward your dream lifestyle is more challenging than it is for someone who is better prepared. Think of the right tools as knowledge about the right resources to use, given your financial situation. And think of skills as your understanding of personal finance. In order to learn about the financial tools and grow your personal finance skills, you'll need financial education.

When I began planning the Road to Financial Wellness tour, I started by talking to friends about the road trip.

I said, "I want to help people understand money. I want to have financial seminars all across the country."

The majority of my friends were excited about the road trip without ever acknowledging the financial education part of it. That was until I had a friend who candidly replied, "I don't know anyone that would take time out of the day to sit in a financial education seminar."

I knew this to be a fact. I knew firsthand that I'd rather be doing something more enjoyable than learning about how I was doing it all wrong.

The opposite is true for self-help seminars—and, dare I say it, get-rich or make-more-money seminars—that oftentimes fill to capacity with people willing to pay to attend. What are these self-styled money seminars offering that financial education seminars do not? They are offering hope for a better tomorrow. They are educating through inspiration, with the underlying promise that by following whatever steps they are selling you can live your dream life.

However, financial education promises exactly the same thing. Being financially educated provides you with the information and skills necessary to make better financial decisions. That in itself can give you hope for your future.

I approach financial education as a form of personal development. Personal financial development is a life-changing skill for improving your life choices specifically as they relate to finances. It is a skill that must be developed and nurtured. Most self-help personal development books are aimed at how you think and challenge you to make improvements to better yourself and your relationships. This book is no different with respect to those goals, as I am challenging you to better your finances and your relationship with money through a shift in mindset. You may have often heard of self-help gurus talking about cultivating a positive mindset. By having a positive mindset, you're able to achieve the goals you've set and overcome whatever insurmountable situation you're facing.

WHAT IS FINANCIAL EDUCATION?

Financial education imparts the ability to understand how money works, how someone can earn or make it, how money is managed, and how it is invested. In more basic terms, financial education brings an understanding of finances, credit, and debt, and how that knowledge can be used to make informed financial decisions. There are many different ways to become financially educated: You can do so by attending classes, watching videos, taking online courses, participating in forums, and reading blogs and books.

The following are a few key reasons financial education is important:

- The burden of retirement planning rests on your shoulders. At work you are given many options to save for retirement, such as 401(k) accounts, stock options, employee stock purchase programs, life insurance, and more.
- As the cost of living increases, wages may stay the same, meaning the need to stretch a dollar becomes increasingly important.
- Today there are more choices in banking products, credit cards, mortgages, and investing products. This increase in the number of financial products can lead to a lot of confusion and bad choices.

■ Additionally, today there are more financial services companies to choose from. Choosing among banks, credit unions, brokerage firms, apps, and financial technology start-ups can be overwhelming.

■ Most important, financial education improves your ability to make sound financial decisions that lead to a higher quality of life.

As I mentioned earlier, most financial education efforts and personal finance discussions remain focused on providing how-to solutions. You can have a manual of how-to information, but if you aren't aware of why that information is needed in your life, then the manual is quite useless. Financial education is power and financial knowledge is influence. Your awareness and application of this knowledge is life changing.

THE ACT PROCESS

The ACT process was created after years of lectures that I had given to help people understand personal finance in a way that would inspire them to act. There are three steps in the process: awareness, creating a plan, and taking control.

Part II of this book covers the Awareness step of the ACT process, which will help you to get clear on where you are and where you want to be as we talk about your values, hopes, and dreams—your vision for your life. This step might be challenging for you, because we're going to talk about your feelings. However, by the end of Part II you'll have gained a better understanding of where you are today, and you'll be able to articulate where you want to be tomorrow. I end that part of the book with what you'll need to know to get you moving along on your road to financial wellness.

Part III, "Creating a Plan," is about budgeting for your dream lifestyle. You'll learn how to identify and set financial goals that align with your values and learn strategies to save better and pay off debt quicker.

Finally, in Part IV, "Taking Control," I'll help you take control of your life with actionable steps and ideas that incorporate your new money mindset to achieve goals focused on saving, spending, and living.

PART II

Awareness

There's a saying that holds that ignorance is bliss—if you don't know about something, you don't need to worry about it. When it comes to your finances, however, ignorance is *not* bliss. The less you know, the more you pay. With financial ignorance, you'll make uninformed financial decisions because you don't know how much income you earn, taxes you pay, monthly expenses you have, or debt you hold. Financial ignorance can lead to banking with the wrong financial institution, choosing the wrong credit card, never investing, and paying more interest and fees than someone who's aware of other options.

On the road trip I would ask attendees about their banking habits.

"How much in fees have you paid in the last year to your bank?" I asked.

"I don't think I pay any fees at all," replied a man from the crowd.

I then asked him, "When was the last time you looked at your bank's fee schedule or looked at your monthly statements?"

"I check my balance daily and get alerts for withdrawals," he stated. "My balance looks correct to me."

"Go check your bank statements right now," I suggested.

Lo and behold, the man who monitored his checking-account balance had been paying a $3 monthly statement fee. The fee went unnoticed because it was small enough to bypass his account-balance monitoring tool.

I was once in exactly the same situation. I was financially ignorant about the amount in fees I was paying for services that I could have received elsewhere for free. After years of financial ignorance and mindless consumption, I finally gained a sense of awareness. I realized I needed to know everything related to my finances. I became financially self-aware.

Self-awareness is having knowledge of your character, beliefs, emotions, and motivations. As you develop self-awareness, you are able to make changes in your thoughts and feelings about yourself, others, and situations. *Financial awareness*, on the other hand, is knowledge of the reality of your finances and clarity about where you are today and where you want to be tomorrow. Combining financial awareness and self-awareness helps you to recognize how you think and feel about money—your money mindset—and provides you with the knowledge to change your financial behaviors. Developing financial self-awareness is a very important skill and is the first step toward controlling your finances so that you can live a wealthy and purposeful life.

Awareness empowered me to make better life and financial decisions. I became more aware of how I wanted to live, what I wanted in life, and why I wanted all these things in the first place. It helped me resolve my savings deficit and my spending problem and shaped my retirement mindset. Financial self-awareness addressed my feelings about money, and that led to a change in my money mindset.

The process of awareness begins with identifying a vision for your life. I'll discuss this in more detail, but basically when you have clarity about your values, hopes, and dreams, you have a framework in which to create a money philosophy. This process will lead to financial self-awareness, which will help you cultivate an improved money mindset that enables you to make better financial decisions to live your dream lifestyle in this lifetime.

The first chapter in this part focuses on your money mindset and challenges you to assess your relationship with money. Subsequent chapters focus on increasing your awareness of where you are today, where you want to be tomorrow, and what you need to know before developing a plan.

CHAPTER **3**

Know Where You're Starting From

Complete this sentence: Money is _____.

Whatever word or words you use to complete this sentence is a good indication of your *money mindset*.

We all carry beliefs about money that got started during childhood and developed over the course of our lives. These beliefs influenced our ideas of what we need and want, what we love and like, and what we deserve. Those ideas taught us what to avoid and what gives us comfort and security.

Everyone has a money mindset. You may not be aware that your current financial situation is a result of this mindset. A money mindset—how you think and feel about money—creates a set of beliefs that determines your behaviors, attitude, and outlook with respect to life and money. It impacts how you manage money and your finances. Your money mindset may often vary from other people's mindsets, because we all have different life experiences that shaped our beliefs about money. Your money mindset may have initially come from your

17

parents and may eventually have been influenced over time by retailers, the media, and the people you've surrounded yourself with.

YOUR MONEY MINDSET

When weighing material desires such as wanting a bigger home, a nicer car, or a dream vacation against the reality of debt, bad credit, or low income, we can end up making decisions that compound our financial problems, preventing us from achieving our goals. Our emotions cannot be separated from money; therefore, we must become more aware of how our emotions impact financial decision making.

Through the process of awareness, I realized that I had held on to money beliefs that were based on a fear of scarcity. I had what's called a *scarcity mindset*, and my financial behavior was based on that thinking. A scarcity mindset is a belief that there isn't enough money to go around, and that money can only be made one way and must be spent before it's taken away. I grew up believing there was not enough money, and that belief became the basis of my spending behavior. I operated with a money philosophy that my paycheck had to be spent entirely and that material goods were the top priority. I did have financial goals, and I had the financial means to achieve them, but my scarcity mindset led me to spend mindlessly and prevented me from reaching my goals.

After a series of financial setbacks and continued dissatisfaction in life, I began a quest to learn more about my relationship with money and to determine whether I was in control of my life, and if not, whether I could regain control of it. I asked myself these three questions:

1. What is my relationship with money?
2. How is my spending contributing to my life?
3. How am I using my time?

Answering these questions increased my understanding of the money beliefs and values I held. This knowledge allowed me to reshape my mindset from one of scarcity to one of abundance. The abundance mindset revolves around the idea that there is plenty of money and many opportunities to make more of it. With a mindset of abundance, you make decisions based on the belief that there is enough money for everyone, making you more mindful of your spending and financial decision making.

WHAT IS YOUR RELATIONSHIP WITH MONEY?

I used to believe that money was important because it represented status and control. I spent money to improve my social status and to show others that I was in control of my life through my ability to spend and with the things I owned.

Money controlled my happiness. I found myself at the mercy of money, hoping it would deliver the satisfaction I sought. I was happy when I had some and stressed when I had none. It was rather an abusive relationship that kept me on an emotional roller coaster. I would anticipate the arrival of my paycheck every other week, and the size of my paycheck determined how happy I was over the weekend. I worked hard for money, but I spent it easily. I traded more hours of my life to earn more money to spend more money to feel no real satisfaction. Through the process of awareness, I realized I was neither in control nor improving my social status. I was digging myself into a deeper financial hole. I wasn't the problem. Money was the problem. This line of thinking made me resent money, and I began believing it to be the root of evil. My feeling toward money increased my disdain for it. Why would I hold on to something so bad? Why would I want to make more of something evil?

Do you think money is evil?

Money is neither good nor evil; however, it can be used for either kind of purpose. While some use money to live their dream lifestyles, there are many others who are controlled by money (as I once was). When you view money as good, not evil, you see money as a tool for change and therefore want to make more of it to positively impact your world. I, however, didn't learn how to make money work for me. I continued to trade my time for money. I learned to fear money, and then I fell under its control.

Does money control you or do you control it?

Think about your current relationship with money and whether it is working for you. Money can conjure up images of abundance or scarcity. Does the thought of money conjure up feelings of fear or empowerment? For many, money elicits fears such as the thought of debt, low wages, and the inability to cover basic needs. A relationship based on fear may cause you to spend more than you make and rely on credit that shackles you to the debt ball and chain.

When money makes you feel empowered, you think about ways to make more of it without exchanging more of your time for it. You're also making sure that you spend it on what adds value in your life, that you save for what's important, and that you invest in assets as income streams.

Do you believe you deserve to be wealthy?

My answer is yes. You deserve to achieve your financial goals and live your dreams. Cultivating an abundance mindset will give you control and enable you to use money as a tool to achieve your goals.

You need to uncover your true feelings about money and how it makes you feel. Be mindful of the words you're using to answer these questions and the thoughts that are coming into your mind. I've found that our initial answers only scratch the surface, so we need to dig deeper. You may find yourself faced with some uncomfortable truths about your relationship with money. Do not shy away from these feelings. Write them down. Don't judge yourself during this discovery phase, either. You are on a fact-finding mission and your goal is understanding, not judgment.

If you come to realize that your money mindset has kept you from achieving your goals, then you have an unhealthy money mindset and it's time to change your money beliefs. In contrast, if you discover that your money mindset has allowed you to live your dream lifestyle, make note of what you're doing right to continue the progress.

 Action

Answer the question, "What is *your* relationship with money?"

HOW IS YOUR SPENDING CONTRIBUTING TO YOUR LIFE?

I knew I had a spending problem. I read books and blogs, attended seminars and workshops, and used many apps to monitor my spending. However, I noticed that my anxiety grew while my spending habits remained unchanged. My problem wasn't due to the size of my paycheck, the interest rates on my credit cards, or the debt I held. It began with the person staring right back at me every time I looked in the mirror. I spent money to feel in control. The more I felt lost in life, the more I spent. This was all in an effort to convince myself that I was in control of something—buying things. I bought things because it was a choice—my choice to spend *my* money. My spending was directed at consumables and depreciating assets and nothing of long-term value. Through awareness I gained understanding, but it took some time before I fully admitted to my unhealthy money mindset that drove my irrational spending behavior.

Here is an indisputable truth: You work to earn money in order to spend money. Whether you decide to spend your paycheck today or later in retirement, you are working to earn money in order to spend it. How you spend, what you spend, and why you spend money have a lot more to do with your money beliefs than simple economics. Based on your money mindset, you value certain items over others because of the worth you give them.

What are you spending on?

I bought things of value. I just didn't buy things that added value in my life. I spent money on things I didn't need and complained that I couldn't afford to invest in things I wanted, such as personal development. Think about the last purchase you made that still provides the same enjoyment as the day it was bought. Likewise, think about the things you want to buy that can have a far greater impact on your quality of life. You might even have a list of things you want to accomplish but have convinced yourself they are financially impossible.

If you're not aware of your values, you may find yourself spending on things that do not matter. When you're investing in yourself, you'll choose to spend on things that improve your situation for the long term, such as new skills, hobbies, and investments. Determine what purchases support your long-term satisfaction and why they are important to you. To gain awareness about your spending mindset, be honest about the emotions that play a key role in what you value and why.

What emotional need are you looking to fill?

We should prioritize spending on things that contribute to our quality of life and help us progress toward our goals. Spending on anything else is a waste of resources. If through answering these questions you discover that you are spending on things of value to you, then it's safe to say you have a healthy money mindset. In contrast, if your spending does little to add value to your life, you have an unhealthy money mindset. You may need to change your spending habits, because not doing so may cause you to rely on credit. Spending without adding value to your life can lead to debt and future financial stress that will weigh on your mind and slow your progress toward your goals.

When you're spending on goods and experiences that don't align with your objectives or add no value in your life you are spending mindlessly. Mindless spending for short-term gratification prevents you from spending on things that matter long-term. This instant gratification may feel good at the moment, but that feeling can also be gone in an instant. Remember, don't stress—you can change your mindset and spend mindfully. I'll show you how in the pages that follow.

 Action

Answer the question, "How is your spending contributing to your life?"

HOW ARE YOU USING YOUR TIME?

I was reckless with my time. I had no concept of its real value: I frequently exchanged my time for more dollars so I could buy more things. I believed time was limitless and that all I needed to do was to work more hours to make more money. The reality is that there are only so many hours in a day and so many days in a week. I eventually reached a limit in terms of my physical health from working so many hours. All those hours worked took a tool on my mental and psychological well-being.

Unfortunately, due to my lack of awareness of my unhealthy money mindset, I began using credit to support my spending. As the credit card balances grew, credit morphed into long-term debt. Debt meant my future time had to be reserved for work and chained me to my job. It became my figurative ball and chain, reminding me that my future did not belong to me.

It would be years later that I would discover that I should focus on increasing the exchange value of my time. However, even that goal needed to evolve to the point at which I would no longer exchange my time for a paycheck. As I increased my awareness and cultivated a healthier money mindset, I began investing time in accumulating assets that generated income streams that freed my time to be used on things that mattered most to me.

Are you treating your time as a valuable finite resource?

Time is the one thing you were born with and the last thing you'll own. Time is the most valuable asset we naturally possess and we exchange this limited resource for money. In fact, the majority of us depend on this exchange for our financial livelihood, but the relationship is one sided. You can always make more money, but you can never make more time. When you have a disregard for your time, you'll find lots of it wasted. Once time is spent, there is no way you can buy it back. Keep this in mind: How you spend your time says a lot about who you are and what's most important to you. Think of your purchases in terms of your time. If you've purchased an $800 smartphone and you make $10 per hour, understand that 80 hours of your life has been spent on that purchase.

Are you investing in yourself?

Your first priority should be your well-being, and that means investing your time to improve your skills and increase your knowledge. The more refined your skills are, the more valuable your time becomes. You don't need to work more hours. You need to invest time to increase your value to command a higher salary. Take a moment right now to assess your relationship with time.

 Action

Answer the question, "How are you using your time?"

CULTIVATE A WEALTHY MONEY MINDSET

It will take time to cultivate a healthier money mindset. You're working to unlearn many of the limiting money beliefs you've held since childhood and undo many of the financial habits you've created. Even small changes in your money beliefs can have a compounding effect on your attitudes, behaviors, and decision making. Progress can and will happen, but you'll need to remain persistent and practice patience and self-awareness.

A wealthy mindset is based on abundance, which can bring peace of mind and help you to gain clarity about a vision for your life. A scarcity mindset is based on fear, which creates barriers that will prevent you from living your dreams. In the following sections you'll learn about the importance of having a vision for your life and how to define a money philosophy to make better financial decisions that align with your values.

On the road to your financial wellness, think of your money mindset as the compass to direct you toward your destination. The better your compass, the smoother your road trip will be. To cultivate a wealthy mentality, fine-tune your compass with the following six fundamental money mindset lessons. We have some limiting beliefs when it comes to money, and although the following advice is nothing new, we need to discuss them in the context of living a purposeful life.

Money Can Buy Happiness

One thing I've learned from the wealthy is that money does buy happiness, and those who understand that concept make better financial decisions. Happiness is not measured by your income or the amount of savings in your bank account. It isn't measured by the size of your home or the features in your car. And it isn't measured by the fancy dinners you eat or the exotic vacations you take. Happiness is a result of realized dreams.

As a child, I never had to worry about shelter, food, or clothing, but I didn't have luxury goods or my own money to spend. I was raised believing money doesn't buy happiness. Money was just a means to exist. That lesson created a mindset with a counterproductive result. I didn't use money as a tool to improve my life. I spent money without awareness of its impact on the life I was living. If money didn't buy happiness, then there was no real purpose in making more of it, aside from defining success based on dollar signs.

However, money can buy happiness in terms of comfort and security. If I spent money mindfully and with purposeful intent, I could positively impact my well-being. I needed to think of money as a tool, not the end goal. Money helps us afford basic human needs, such as housing, food, medicine, and clothing. If you lack money to pay for these needs it is more challenging to live comfortably. As a result, you can find yourself more stressed about your situation. When you make more money, you can afford additional comforts in your life, and with awareness you're able to make financial decisions that align with your values.

Knowing that money can buy happiness can make it easier for you to choose long-term happiness over short-term satisfaction.

Live Your Dreams, Not Someone Else's

During the height of the real estate bubble, my parents decided to remodel their home. My parents weren't alone in the neighborhood. It seemed at the time that everyone on my block was improving their house's curb appeal.

"You're keeping up with the Joneses," said the mailman to me after I signed for a package.

It was the first time I'd heard this phrase, and I wondered where in the neighborhood the Joneses lived. The Joneses, I soon learned, were not a literal family down the block but a statement referring to a desire to enjoy a social status comparable to our neighbors. I am not sure if my parents' desire to remodel came from a desire to keep up with our neighbors. But as I soon learned, it did stem from the general idea at that time of doing what others were doing: Improving their homes to raise their real estate value.

Keeping up with the Joneses is a vicious cycle that never ends. In fact, as you try to keep up with your Joneses, those Joneses (i.e., other people) are trying to keep up with their own Joneses, too. Instead of worrying about what others are doing with their money, you should only be concerned with how you're using yours. Don't work harder to get what everyone else has, because that isn't going to bring you happiness. The stress of keeping up with the Joneses will add to your continued dissatisfaction. You may find yourself financing items to preserve social status and end up compounding the financial stress that you're feeling.

Don't try to keep up with the Joneses, but *do* keep your vision and goals in mind when making purchases that add value in your life. If you attempt to keep up with the Joneses, you've actually given other people control of how you spend your money. You won't be spending money on your dreams; you'll be spending it to live theirs.

Don't Inflate Your Lifestyle

Lifestyle inflation is increasing your spending at the rate at which your income increases. You might be thinking the obvious: We earn more so we can spend more. However, if it remains unchecked, lifestyle inflation can prevent you from reaching your financial goals. It keeps you in the cycle, unable to pursue dreams because you need to continue to work just to pay your bills.

You might tell yourself that you'll start your emergency fund after that annual salary increase you're expecting. Or you'll begin to contribute to your company's 401(k) plan after a promotion. You might even convince yourself that a higher-paying job is the only solution to getting out of debt. However, because of lifestyle inflation, you may still find it difficult to achieve these financial goals because you're spending $75,000 at the same rate you spent your $35,000 salary.

When I was making minimum wage, I was able to afford the things I needed but dreamed of buying the things I wanted. As my income grew to four times the minimum wage rate, I noticed the things I wanted became things I needed. What seemed like luxuries at one point in time became standard, so I sought more expensive wants. I didn't realize at the time I was experiencing lifestyle inflation. The cost of my lifestyle was increasing at the same rate as my income. I went from a reliable used car to a new Toyota Camry to a BMW 3 Series coupe to fill the need for transportation. The more I made, the more willing I was to pay a higher price for new luxuries.

There is nothing wrong with wanting luxury goods and spending money on them; however, if it keeps you from achieving your goals, then it is a problem. If your lifestyle is inflating, then you are going to find it difficult to save money, get out of debt, and invest in your retirement.

The Purchase of Things and Experiences
Is the Same Thing

There are studies that have found that spending money on experiences has a far greater impact on your happiness than spending on things. Experiences have a profound effect on how we view the quality of our lives, whereas things have a depreciating effect on our happiness. Even with this disparity, experiences and things are similar in that there's a cost to both. You're either spending money on things or spending time on experiences. For many of us, however, experiences trump things.

Let's try an exercise.

Think of an item you bought recently because you absolutely loved it. Do you feel the same level of happiness as when you first made the purchase? You might realize you don't feel the same and have become indifferent toward it.

Now, can you think of a memorable experience with a loved one you've had? What are you feeling right now? Do you find yourself smiling? If you're feeling a sense of happiness, that's because remembering experiences can help you relive that moment.

There are situations when things can add to the experience. When I owned my BMW, it was quite an experience driving through the winding roads of Napa Valley as the car smoothly accelerated and hugged the curves. As I think of that experience, I reminisce happily about those moments.

Whether you decide to spend your money on the finer things in life or spend it traveling around the world, spend on things that matter to you. You can spend money on expensive clothes, luxury brands, or a backpacking trip just as long as you understand how your purchase supports your vision for your life.

Wealth Is Not Measured by How Much You Spend
but by How Much You've Saved

Wealth is being popularized as a state of mind, but I want to focus on wealth from an economic perspective, as the abundance of money. Wealth is not how much you make or how much you spend. If the ability to spend money determined wealth, I would have been considered wealthy a very long time ago. Having wealth means you have more than enough money to cover your living expenses now and well into the future. Wealth is calculated based on how much cash you've saved and the investments and properties you have.

For example, a person who makes $50,000 a year and is saving half of her salary can be wealthier than a person who makes $100,000 and only saves 10 percent of his salary. During a lecture at a manufacturing company in Menlo Park, California, a production-line employee making $55,000 a year shared that he owned two homes, had an emergency fund, contributed to the company's 401(k) plan, carried no debt, and was on track for retirement. He attributed his financial well-being to saving as much as possible of what he makes. This is the complete opposite of a managing director from Boston, who told me he was making $115,000 a year but couldn't find an extra dollar to save toward his children's college fund. After going through his income and expenses, he saw that his spending was outpacing his income. He came to the conclusion that he just needed more money.

Accumulating wealth can be a result of purposeful living. You may find that when you have a vision for your life, you are spending less and saving more. You are able to cover your financial obligations and still have money left over. You don't have a dire need to work in order to pay your bills. This frees up your time to focus on the things that matter most to you: Achieving your dreams.

Make it a priority to build your wealth. In accumulating wealth, you are not limited by your income but by your mindset about how it can be achieved. Keep your living expenses way below your means, spend less, and save more and invest in things that appreciate in value. Again, be mindful of lifestyle inflation and spending habits related to the Joneses that impact your ability to become wealthy.

Make Yourself a Priority and Pay Yourself First

I can still recall working 78 hours in one workweek at a job I had at Newark Airport. To work this many hours, I slept in an office that was located underneath the airport terminal near the baggage loading area. I served drinks in the first-class lounge, helped with chartered flight check-in, and loaded bags into the planes. I'd nap for a few hours, wake up, and take on another shift. I remember being excited to get my paycheck that week, since I would have some money left over after my bills were paid. However, the reality quickly set in: After taxes, distributions, and bill payments, I was left with zero dollars in my bank account. I had no cash left to spend, and that week became the last time I worked that many hours in exchange for a paycheck.

I didn't realize at the time that by prioritizing everything else except saving money, I was becoming increasingly dissatisfied with my job. My performance suffered, my work relationships deteriorated, and I eventually lost my job.

You might have had a similar experience, or maybe you're just living paycheck to paycheck. Maybe saving money is something you know you need to do but believe is impossible to accomplish. There is nothing motivating about working day in and day out, only to see the paycheck direct deposited in your checking account gone by the end of the payday. I have learned that saving even a small part of your paycheck every payday can help cultivate a healthy money mindset.

Paying yourself first doesn't mean spending on whatever it is you want. It means saving money. You may be tempted to pay all your bills, leaving you with nothing to save. Paying your bills is necessary; however, to keep motivated, you need to make some positive financial gains. To accomplish this, think of yourself as a monthly expense that needs to get paid, the same as your cellphone bill. Each payday you must transfer a small amount into a savings account. The amount can be as little as $5 or up to an amount that is financially doable and can be consistently saved each payday. The benefit to saving any amount is building and reinforcing a savings habit. The next step is executing a purposeful savings strategy, which will be covered later in this book.

In the next chapter we'll discuss the importance of knowing where you want to go, and we'll help you clarify your values, set a vision for your life, and create a guiding money philosophy.

CHAPTER **4**

Know Where You Want to Go

When I was a kid, I had a vision for the life I wanted to live. Somewhere along the path to adulthood, I replaced the life that I wanted to live with the things that I wanted to own. I could tell you I wanted to own a home and a luxury car, but I had a hard time articulating a vision for my life. This lack of vision contributed to my disregard for time. That disregard led to a compulsion to spend more on things in order to resolve my conflict over my time not being used for something more purposeful.

No amount of spending and borrowing or saving and investing will get you what you want if you're not clear about what you really value and what you're working toward.

If you don't know where you're headed, then you can't expect to reach your destination. On the road to your financial wellness, you need to know where you're going and what it is that you want. As you work to improve your compass—your money mindset—it's time to figure out where you want to go. Think of your values as the gas in your car, your vision for your life as your destination, and your money philosophy as the rules of the road. The steps you need to take in figuring out where you want to go are as follows:

1. Clarify your values and know what is important to you.
2. Have a vision for your life based on all your hopes and dreams.
3. Have a money philosophy to guide your financial principles.

CLARIFY YOUR VALUES

On the Road to Financial Wellness tour, I asked thousands of attendees at events across the country a fundamental question—what brings happiness into their lives? This question made people uncomfortable. I could feel the energy in the room change. Some of the event attendees would look downward to avoid eye contact with me, and others stared intently while holding their breath, waiting for me to give them an answer.

I would purposely pause for an extended period of time as I scanned the room.

At one event in Denver, Colorado, the silence was interrupted by a 25-year-old college student who asked, "What does this have to do with financial education?"

"It has a lot more to do with personal finance than you think," I responded.

This question about happiness *is* hard for many people to answer. You may actually find you're unable to give an immediate answer to that question. You might even scoff at the notion that happiness has anything to do with financial education. Or if you're like some of the event attendees you could have given the same answer they did: more money. However, as I mentioned earlier, money is a tool. It is not the end goal.

What brings happiness into your life?

Take a moment to think about this.

Do you have an answer? This question is asking you to think about the things, people, places, hobbies, and experiences that make you happy. You can bring happiness into your life by doing more of the things you value. However, if you aren't clear about your values, you're most likely spending on things that do not matter.

We're often taught to set financial goals first, without going through the process of clarifying our values. The conventional belief is that once you set and achieve your financial goals you'll have the ideal life, and that maintaining that lifestyle will become your purpose. Or, in effect, that values are the result of achieving financial goals and not the reason for them.

In my case, I achieved financial milestones, but then eventually realized I was living a lifestyle I didn't want to. Through the process of awareness, I discovered bigger problems that prevented me from living my dream lifestyle. I was making financial decisions contrary to the values I held. I said travel experiences, for example, were important to me and yet with every paycheck I always had a reason to spend on other things. How I spent my money reflected what I valued.

What do you value?

You might list a number of things, such as family, security, health, education, and community. However, take a look at the items you've bought recently and at the things you surround yourself with. I can determine what's most important to you based on how you spend your money.

If you are like many people I've met, you're probably spending money on things that don't align with what you value. It's important to identify and clarify your values first and then spend accordingly.

During the event in Denver I continued the conversation with the college student about what he valued.

"I value money," said the college student.

I asked, "What is it about money you value?"

"So I can afford the things I want," he responded.

"What is it that you want?" I countered.

"I want my own place," he added, "and I need to get a car."

This isn't an unusual response. In most cases, I would ask a further clarifying question: Why do you want your own place or need a new car? And the response would typically only scratch the surface. In this particular case, the college student stated that he wanted his privacy and a reliable car.

As the conversation progressed I asked a series of whys, and he finally admitted he wanted to "feel like an adult" and "have more freedom" to do what he wanted.

"This idea of freedom you have," I said, "is about being able to do as you wish, but the more bills and expenses you have, the less freedom you'll actually have. You'll spend more time working than enjoying whatever it is you enjoy. Figure out what's really important and then determine how you can get your privacy and your car without sacrificing what you really value—your freedom."

For many people talking about money is difficult enough, so adding a discussion about how money makes them feel is nearly impossible. However, it is an important conversation that will help you clarify your values.

To figure out what you value, begin by describing your ideal lifestyle. Start with the basics such as shelter, food, health, and clothing. Become aware of the feelings you have toward these basic needs. Then answer this question: Why are these needs important to me? Take the time to write down your answers.

Continue asking a series of whys to increase your awareness of what you actually value: Why do you value this item? Why do you want or need it? Why is the desire to own or have this item so strong? Why will you choose this over something else? And so on.

Let me expand on this explanation by using an example of something that I value and often hear from others that they value too: traveling more. Using this example, define why traveling is important to you. How does it lead to a better quality of life? Remember, it's not about the place you'll visit or the experience you'll gain, but what those places and moments mean in your life. Most answers I receive regarding the desire to travel are related to creating new memories and having new experiences. Other times this desire has to do with breaking the daily routine or finding a temporary escape. Why do you want a break from your routine? Why do you need to escape? From the answers you give, you may find that what you're really looking for isn't a break from your routine but an actual change of lifestyle. In that case your financial goals and financial decisions must be based on planning for that lifestyle change, not on planning your vacation.

Asking these whys will help you gain clarity about your values. This increased awareness of your values will improve your financial decision making to ensure that you're cultivating your dream lifestyle.

Action

Write down what you value on a piece of paper and circle your top three items. Choose the first circled item and begin asking yourself a series of questions that ask why you value that thing. Get clear on why you value one thing before proceeding to the next circled item.

HAVE A VISION FOR YOUR LIFE

If you only live once, what is your vision of a purposeful life? A vision takes all your thoughts and feelings and all your hopes and dreams and uses them to shape a meaningful life—a life filled with wealth and purpose. The vision for your life isn't a list of financial goals or life milestones. It is your big picture—the conditions under which your life takes place—aligned with your values. When you're progressing toward living your vision for your life, you're living your dream lifestyle.

Do you have a vision for your life?

Take a moment to think about this.

If you're finding it difficult to envision your dream lifestyle, you may be fixated on your current financial situation. You can't envision your tomorrow if your mind is preoccupied with just making it through the day. On the road to your financial wellness, a vision is the final destination you've chosen as the ideal state of living.

If you still have a mental block, ask yourself this additional question: *If I had no debt or financial obligations, how would I spend my time?*

Keep in mind that how you spend your time is the lifestyle you're actually living. For example, you may believe you're living a luxurious lifestyle because you drive a fancy car and wear brand-name clothing, but you might also be spending most of your time working to pay for those lifestyle choices. The actual lifestyle you're living may not be as luxurious as it seems; rather, it's a workcentric lifestyle. Consider this: If the majority of your time is allocated to working more hours to afford, rather than enjoy, your luxuries, then those luxury goods are just coping mechanisms. They are purchases to deal with the reality of your workcentric lifestyle.

Define your vision. It will give you clarity about your direction in life. It will help you make better life choices and better financial decisions that support living the dream lifestyle that is your destination.

Think of the lifestyle you want to live. Can you articulate the details of that lifestyle? What elements does it include? What qualities of those elements make you feel happy? I've found most of us answer these questions based on how others define an ideal lifestyle or what we've been programmed to believe is one. Such a lifestyle may conflict with the one you actually envision.

We continue to confuse our lifestyle with the things we own or the job we have. It's ingrained in us to think of life as a series of financial milestones. This causes us to believe that life is a checklist of financial goals: pay for college, get your first job with a real salary, get a mortgage and own a home, pay for a wedding, set up your kids' college funds, invest for retirement, and so on. We think that being able to add more things to that list and checking them off when we achieve them are indicators of success, but that's not the case.

Do you earn money doing something you don't enjoy?

I've been fortunate in that I've enjoyed the majority of the jobs I've had. However, my satisfaction with them tended to come and go. At peak dissatisfaction I would spend a big portion of my paycheck to alleviate the pain of working too many hours doing things I didn't like. After I decided to leave my senior executive job, many people stated that I needed to keep my job and just buy a house.

I found it difficult to share my dreams with people. So instead I told them, "I just don't know what I want." That was probably a very true statement at the time. As an adult, saying I was lost seemed to be more acceptable than sharing my dreams like a child.

One of my friends advised me, "Owning a house is a better use of your money. At least you'll have something to show for it." I thought about this for some time, and I actually began searching for homes online. But as I continued to grow in awareness and made more money, the thought of owning a home—potentially a smart financial move—made no sense to me.

I wanted to find a purpose for my life. At the time I didn't know what that was, but I knew I didn't want my life's purpose to be paying off a mortgage. As I freed myself from my financial obligations I was able to clear my mind and answer my whys, which led to my vision statement: *The vision for my life is freedom to pursue work of positive social impact anywhere around the world.*

That vision has enabled me to come to the realization that owning a home or a car are not goals I need to have, because they would prevent me from pursuing work I enjoy and traveling more freely.

While on the road trip, my colleagues and I asked people about their dreams, and I learned that many people had difficulty sharing them. It was much easier for them to talk about finances than it was to talk about the vision for their lives. For most, the problem was their lack of vision to begin with, which made it challenging for them to answer the question in the first place.

"What is your dream lifestyle?" I'd ask.

"Don't worry about my dreams," replied a man from the audience. "Just tell me how I should invest in my 401(k)."

"I'm sure a financial advisor can tell you what you should do and how you should do it, but I'd recommend that you figure out why you're investing in the first place," I responded.

I've had similar discussions with other people throughout the country. Many wanted a plan from a professed expert without having to explain why they wanted to invest. I would caution that if you don't know the reasons you're saving or investing, then that's a bigger issue that must be addressed before any type of plan is created.

Why do you want to invest? If your response to this question is to prepare for retirement, you're not alone. It seems most people in my seminars respond to that question by stating that retirement is their number one financial goal.

"Retirement is a lifestyle where your income is coming from your savings and investment returns rather than from a paycheck from a job. With a vision and proper planning, that can be achieved sooner than age 70," I'd state.

I would continue the discussion by asking, "What do you want to do in retirement?"

While some people would just respond that they wouldn't be able to retire, many more would begin to answer that question. I prompted those who could imagine their retirements to become clearer in their visions for their retirement lives.

"How are you exactly going to spend your time?" I would ask.

The answers became much more interesting and colorful. I then challenged the group to start planning to retire sooner to live that lifestyle.

Do you find it difficult to share your dream lifestyle?

If you find it difficult to share your vision for your life, it's probably because as life happens, we simply accept as fate that our dreams will never become reality. However, as I continue to have these conversations with people, the main reason that most can't talk about their dreams is that they're preoccupied with thoughts of their finances: credit card payments, student loans, monthly rent, the need to finance a car, and how they'll ever be able to retire. To think about dreams causes anxiety, so we avoid it.

And yet I argue for the importance of having a vision for your life. You need to have a clear idea of the life you're working toward. You need this vision to help identify your financial goals and to motivate you to make the right decisions to achieve them.

If you have a vision for your life, you could be doing work you love for a lot less money and have more free time to pursue other interests that align with your values. Again, the vision for your life is how you hope to live—your greatest version of you.

 Action

Define your vision for your life. What do you envision doing with your time? What are your hopes and dreams? Where do you want to live? Who do you want to spend your time with? What do you hope to accomplish? Create a personal vision statement from these answers.

FOLLOW A MONEY PHILOSOPHY

I've had many wishes. I've hoped for many things. I've also had many dreams. But it took some time for me to turn my dreams into a vision for living. As I became aware of what really mattered to me it became easier for me to follow a money philosophy that aligned with my values to help me live my dream lifestyle in this lifetime.

A vision for your life will keep you focused and motivated to spend your time and money on the things that matter to you. A money philosophy will help you make better financial decisions. On the path to financial wellness, think of this philosophy as the rules of the road that will help you reach your destination safely and enjoyably.

Many people follow a philosophy of living, whether they are aware of it or not. It guides them on health, work, family, and relationships. For example, your philosophy about health may cause you to eat well, exercise, and sleep often—or it may have the opposite effect and cause you not to mind what you eat just as long as you're eating something tasty. A money philosophy is made up of the guiding principles with which you manage your finances and make financial decisions that align with your values and support your vision. It makes saving and spending decisions simpler and easier. I didn't always have a money philosophy— it wasn't until what I valued became clear to me that I began following guidelines on how I would use money. I realized that I value experiences and friendships over things, so I created a money philosophy to prioritize social activities over material consumption. I didn't want to be tied to one location; I wanted to have the ability to explore the world without the worry of a house or car. My money philosophy values renting over ownership. I rent an apartment and I haven't owned a car since 2011.

I value freedom and my money philosophy is that of minimalism. After realizing that I had a mystifying emotional connection to an area rug that I had sold on Craigslist, I questioned my attachment to things and the space they occupied in my mind. The less I owned, the less thought I gave to inanimate objects. This was good for my creativity and my bank account. Additionally, this money philosophy of minimalism is reflected in my preference to have items that are functional and usable instead of brand new and pristine.

If I were offered a new car without a car loan, my answer would be, "Thank you, but I don't want one." Who would turn down a free car? I would—because my money philosophy would remind me that a car has ownership costs, such as insurance, maintenance, registration fees, and the potential for parking tickets.

The principles I follow have really helped me with a wide array of decisions, but I'm mindful that my philosophy can change if and when my vision for my life changes.

Without a money philosophy, you might do something today that undoes what you did the day before. You might find it difficult to manage your finances in line with your values effectively, leading you to spend mindlessly on things and experiences that are not important to you. Your money philosophy is based on the guiding principles that ensure that your long-term satisfaction is prioritized over short-term gratification. Before proceeding, contemplate your money philosophy. If you realize you don't have a specific money philosophy, the following chapters will help you develop guiding principles through changes in your financial behaviors and habits.

 Action

Create a set of three financial principles aligned with your values to simplify your financial decision making and improve your life.

CHAPTER **5**

Getting What You Want

went from having dreams to owning things. I spent cash and used credit to overcome my scarcity mindset, and still found myself unable to curb my spending or allocate more money to savings. When cash became tight my credit usage became habitual, turning credit into long-term debt.

We spend rather than save because our future needs are unknown and instant gratification serves a current emotional need. When underlying emotions are not addressed, the spending continues uninterrupted, solidifying the habit. Spending habitually without thought can lead to inconsistent financial decisions that impact your long-term satisfaction.

Since you've grown in awareness about your money mindset, your values, and your vision for life, it's now time to improve your financial behaviors and change your habits.

CHANGE YOUR FINANCIAL BEHAVIORS AND HABITS

On the road to financial wellness you may need to change your behaviors and habits, just as you might change parts in a car before an actual road trip. As you gain awareness about your values, create your vision, and define your money philosophy, you'll need to challenge old financial habits that were created from your previously held money beliefs. These habits may be good or bad. This chapter will help you to increase your awareness of the good habits that help you with money and to change the bad habits that prevent you from achieving your goals.

THE HABIT OF SPENDING

I had a morning ritual: Every day I drank a freshly brewed hazelnut-flavored coffee and ate a toasted bagel with cream cheese. Coffee and a bagel was a breakfast that I enjoyed. I certainly wasn't breaking the bank, so I never thought of this ritual in any financial context. That was until I attended a meeting that challenged that mindset.

The morning of that meeting, I was running late and decided to take a different road to work. Instead of going to my usual coffee shop, I stopped at the Starbucks on the corner and bought my second-favorite coffee-flavored drink: a caramel Frappuccino. I walked into the meeting and found every seat was taken except for one seat in the front row. The topic of the meeting, I would soon discover, was budgeting.

"Are you a Starbucks-loving apartment renter or a Folgers Crystals homeowner?" asked the presenter.

I sat there staring intently into the eyes of the presenter, hoping he wouldn't notice the Starbucks coffee I had been drinking since he began speaking. I stopped making eye contact for fear I was making my thoughts too obvious. I looked down instead at my right hand, which was holding that clear coffee cup with my misspelled name, and I asked myself, "Is this why I am an apartment renter?"

Assuming there were 262 weekdays in the year in which I spend $4.50 each morning, I spent $1,179 on coffee and bagels. That amount certainly wouldn't be enough to buy a home, but it made me realize that I needed to take a look at how I was living my life. I wanted for the very first time to uncover financial behaviors and habits that were preventing me from achieving my goals.

I realized I was doing everything wrong. I was habitually and mindlessly spending. I wasn't spending my money on Starbucks coffee each and every day, but I was spending on other habits. The presenter's question didn't suggest that my morning ritual was wrong, but it caused me to start thinking about whether my habits had any financial implications for achieving long-term goals. It made me want to increase my awareness of little spending habits, which eventually led to a desire to challenge larger monthly expenses.

I am not advocating that you stop spending on rituals that are enjoyable for you. However, I did eventually stop my daily morning-coffee-and-bagel routine. On occasion, I do indulge myself, but it's something I've gained a greater appreciation for as a treat rather than as a routine. I also found the extra cash I needed to start my emergency fund.

Again, I am not against spending. In fact, I want you to spend— if, and only if, you're purchasing something you love. You're trading your most valuable asset—time—for money, and to buy things that add no value is a waste of your life. If Starbucks coffee or a morning routine gives you comfort, then figure out how you can afford that expense, because it adds value in your life. Since you only live once, make sure you're spending on things that matter to you.

 Action

Evaluate your daily, weekly, and monthly routines. *Challenge every purchase you make.*

Ask yourself a series of questions similar to the following:

- How are you spending your money?
- What are you spending it on?

Can you identify spending that is based on habit? Do you need morning coffee? Do you binge watch Netflix? Are you gassing up your car with premium gasoline? Are you paying for recurring monthly services?

THE HABIT OF SAVING

Our money mindset isn't limited to impacting how we spend; it also has an effect on our desire to save. The vast majority of people should be able to save a portion of their paychecks, but their money beliefs prevent them from taking any meaningful steps to make it happen. *Are your money beliefs keeping you from saving money?*

We are taught early in our lives that everything has a price and that in order to get anything we must spend money. This philosophy has enabled the habit of spending to flourish and has reinforced the belief that spending is more rewarding than saving money.

At one event that I had during the Road to Financial Wellness tour, a woman from North Carolina shared that she's never saved a single dollar in her life. Although she knew why it was important to save money, she was quite ashamed of the fact that she'd never had a savings account and didn't know how to "really" save money. You might feel the same way and believe that the only way to start saving is to make more money first. I challenge you to think otherwise.

"I just don't make enough money," exclaimed the 30-year-old.

I replied, "Well, you can save money, even if it's one dollar."

Without missing a beat, she responded, "How can a dollar make a difference?" It was a rhetorical question, because who in their right mind would save just one dollar?

The fact is, one dollar *can* make a difference. Saving your first dollar when you haven't saved a day in your life is a life-altering move. With that small gesture, you've broken the tight hold of your limiting money mindset. You've cracked your impenetrable spending habit. That one dollar you purposefully saved is the first stone you've laid in the foundation of your savings habit.

About six months after the event, I received an e-mail from the 30-year-old who had never saved a day in her life. She now had an emergency fund of over $1,000. Her method: an automatic payroll transfer each payday of $5 from her checking account to a savings account.

She realized the money transferred into the savings account wasn't missed. She took one small step and then made incremental increases to her payday transfers. She now transfers $50 per payday and adds extra money whenever she makes overtime.

That small step in the other direction can loosen the grasp of your unhealthy spending habit. Because spending feels more rewarding, we've cultivated a belief that our current spending in relation to our income is satisfactory and what needs to change in order to save money is to make more money. Maybe you'll save when you get your annual merit-based increase or when you get that promotion. Maybe you'll start saving when you get the holiday bonus or get your tax refund. Without a habit of saving, you'll find any excuse to continue spending as before when faced with these scenarios.

Are you saving money? How are you saving money? What's preventing you from saving just one dollar per paycheck? Further along in this book I will introduce you to a savings strategy called purposeful savings that will align your savings goals with your vision for your life.

 Action

Start the habit of saving and set up an automatic transfer from your checking account into a savings account each payday. Don't have a savings account? Open an account by making the initial minimum deposit required and then set up an automatic transfer.

GET IN THE KNOW

We've lived far too long in the land of the unknown; now it's time to get in the know. As you continue to grow in awareness, it's important to increase your understanding of your money beliefs to help you make the necessary changes in your behaviors and habits. The more you know, the better equipped you'll be to make financial decisions that help you live your dream lifestyle in this lifetime.

As you continue along the road to financial wellness there are some key things you need to know. In this section we'll continue to discuss the importance of your money mindset and values in reshaping your relationship with money. I'll also further explain the importance of knowing the following areas in empowering you to make changes:

- How you spend
- The difference between needs and wants
- Credit as a financial tool
- The power of time
- Your financial numbers

Know How You Spend

Have you ever made yourself believe you needed something? Your thoughts are consumed by the desire to own the item. You feel you can't live without it and you must have it soon.

Then the phone rings or a friend visits.

After some time has passed, you ask yourself what it was that you were searching for online. What was it that you absolutely needed moments ago but now can't even remember?

This is a good example of mindless spending. You were about to make a purchase that really didn't matter to you or add any value in your life.

There are many ways to mindlessly spend on what we believe we need and what we think we want. You might have a belief that you need more, unaware of the fact that you wouldn't be able to use it all in your lifetime.

You can also mindlessly spend on big-ticket items like houses and cars. For example, you may believe that you need a larger home or a larger car and assume you have a need for the extra space it will provide. However, you haven't determined what value this larger item will actually provide to you. A financial consequence may be larger maintenance expenses than would be incurred for a home or a car that is more appropriate for your actual needs.

Increase your awareness of how you spend to understand the changes needed to improve your financial situation. The more you know about how and why you spend, the more control you'll have over your life. The next four sections will look at common forms of spending mindlessly: habit spending, retail therapy, brand-loyalty spending, and bargain hunting.

Habit Spending

Habit spending occurs because you have ingrained spending behaviors that are habitual in nature, which you may not even be aware you have. These habits were created from your money beliefs, which have perpetuated your current financial situation.

Have you ever found yourself buying goods because they helped you cope with an emotional low? Are you buying certain brands just because they're what you're used to wearing, or are you shopping for bargains because that's the only way you feel in control?

Habit spending can be as simple as buying a morning coffee at Starbucks or buying premium gas at the pump. Or your habit spending may be more complex, such as continuing to pay monthly fees for banking services or insurance premiums. Or you may have a smoking habit or maintain an organic food diet. You've accepted these expenses as is and don't think to question them. However, it's important to review them in order to change the habits that are not healthy and promote the habits that add value to your life.

I had a conversation with a colleague and friend of mine about spending. He shared how proud he was that he didn't have a daily lunch habit like most of his coworkers, who ate out each and every workday.

"I don't eat at the cafeteria every day or go out for lunch," my friend stated.

"What do you eat, then?" I asked.

"Well, I don't really have a set time for lunch, but I'll eat when I'm hungry. I don't spend as much as others," he said.

"How much do you spend for food throughout a workday?" I asked.

"I don't know exactly, but it's probably less than $5 a day," he replied.

"Let's do an experiment," I suggested.

I instructed him to continue his pattern for 30 days, but requested that he use a debit card during this period so we could monitor his spending habits. After the allotted time period ended, he was surprised to learn that he spent an average of $14.50 a day on food. That was almost three times higher than he believed he spent daily on food. During the first few days of the experiment his food expenses were under $8 a day, which can probably be attributed to the fact that he was more mindful of his spending early on. As the awareness of the experiment waned, he became less mindful and his existing spending habits reemerged. He may not have been eating lunch regularly, but he was habitual in spending on snacks and fast food at irregular times. What surprised him was how many times he bought snacks at the gas station's convenience store every day—something that he didn't even realize that he was doing.

Are you aware of how you spend? For example, do you drive to work instead of using public transportation? Do you consistently buy bottled water? Do you forget to turn off the lights when you leave a room? Do you keep the AC or heat on when you leave the house?

 Action

Think about your lunch habit. Do you prepare your lunch at home? Or do you eat lunches out? Determine how many times a week you eat lunches that weren't prepared by you. What is the cost of your lunch habit? Apply this method to other habits you uncover.

Retail Therapy

Are you surfing websites and making random online purchases when you feel sad, lonely, or depressed? Do you head out to the mall or the supermarket whenever you feel out of control?

Retail therapy is buying goods, services, and experiences to make you feel better. It's mood enhancing. Retail therapy provides you with a temporary feeling of control.

I admit that I used retail therapy to combat some of my dissatisfaction with my life and to deal with my crumbling financial situation. I traveled often for work and I found myself killing time by walking around at shopping malls. I didn't realize it at the time, but I was giving myself retail therapy because I was unhappy. I spent money to feel better, and I found myself buying things that I didn't need or even want. It just gave me a feeling of control.

During a trip to Dallas, Texas, I felt especially lonely. I drove to the mall and spent a few hundred dollars on clothes and shoes. I recall telling myself that these were great finds because I got things I wanted on sale and at a discount. I bought so many things that I needed to buy another piece of luggage to bring them home.

Then came an eye-opening experience: I realized that I didn't unpack the suitcase containing my new clothes and shoes for over a month. It had remained collecting dust in my walk-in closet.

Since I felt helpless and not in control of my situation, the one thing I could control was making a purchase. It was up to me to decide if I wanted or didn't want something. Even though at times I didn't have the money to make a purchase, I relied on credit to make it. As my financial situation deteriorated, I found myself using retail therapy once again to combat my feeling of helplessness. The more financial stress I felt, the more I spent, which compounded my financial troubles.

Do you find yourself spending because of an emotional need? If you find yourself using retail therapy to cope with your emotional roller coaster, you might try an experiment that worked for me. To get a sense of control and feel the instant gratification that I was looking for, I'd buy whatever it was I wanted, but I wouldn't open it or use it. After a day or two, I'll ask myself if the purchase I'd made was something I truly wanted. Oftentimes I found the act of purchasing something provided the retail therapy I desired, while the product itself was something I didn't want. In those cases I returned the unopened packages.

Eventually the frequent shopping and returning of unused items made me aware of my retail-therapy spending. That awareness allowed me to change my coping strategy during low emotional moments.

 Action

Grab an item you bought recently and answer the question, what's my purpose for buying this item? What am I feeling right now?

Brand-Loyalty Spending

As I continued on my path to awareness, I began questioning all my purchasing behaviors. I came to the conclusion that my brand loyalty was based on an emotional need to be desirable to others. I drove a BMW because it made me feel sexier. I wore expensive brand-name clothes because they made me feel better. I only used products from Apple because it supported a narrative I wanted to promote—that I was trendy and cool.

My brand-loyalty habit was how I defined myself. I was making my purchasing decisions not based on quality (although brand names can definitely be associated with high quality), but because these brands symbolized the person I believed I was.

I will admit I didn't know who I was back then. I was living a lifestyle that I didn't recognize. I didn't know my values or what really mattered to me. I didn't have a vision for my life. I had the financial means, and spending my hard-earned money on brand names helped me cope with my actual situation. I may not have felt successful inside, but I sure would promote the image of success with the clothes I wore and the products I used.

I learned something quite interesting. When we don't know who we are, we use the names of others to express our identity to the world. This statement summarizes my current belief that a lack of self-awareness makes us more prone to use brand names and company logos to explain to others what we stand for and what we value.

Through self-awareness, I know what brands I like and what brands I don't. The value I give them isn't based on what has been marketed or socially promoted to me. I've learned that the value brands have is the value I give them. I am more mindful of the brands I buy that align with my values. And I make sure that I always have the money to purchase them.

Companies (and society) can say that brand X represents Y, but if you don't believe it or don't buy into the value being marketed, then the brand represents nothing. Don't be fooled into believing that a brand makes you any more or any less of a person.

Ask yourself these questions when you're buying brand names:

- Do you make purchases because you're loyal to particular brands?
- What do those labels or company names mean to you?
- Is a higher price tag worth the expense?
- Can you define yourself by other means?

 Action

Think about the brands of the car you drive, the clothes you're wearing now, and the smartphone you have. How do those brands represent your values?

Bargain Hunting

A few years ago, when I was conducting a lecture on spending habits outside Raleigh, North Carolina, I was confronted by someone who disagreed with my thoughts on bargain shopping.

"If it's a bargain, it would be foolish not to make the purchase. I may not need it now but I may need it later. Isn't it better to buy it on sale so I have it when I do need it?" the man asked.

I nodded and replied, "What have you purchased recently that fits this scenario?"

"I bought a brand-new drivable lawnmower. It was 65 percent off, since it was last year's model," he said.

"Was your current lawnmower broken?" I asked.

"No, it isn't; but it's old, so it could go anytime," he responded.

A year later, I went back to Raleigh to give a second lecture, and the same man approached me and said, "You know, I still have two lawnmowers in my garage. They both work fine. I've been using both because it bothered me that one was collecting dust."

I asked, "So what do you plan to do with them?"

"I'm at the point where I want to get rid of the old one," the man replied, "because I can't even fit my car in the garage."

Do you find yourself buying goods because you perceive a future need for them? How do you determine the probability that this need will arise?

There may also be times when you find yourself actively searching for a bargain. However, you may be proactively seeking discounts to validate a purchase that's actually unnecessary. You may tell yourself that the purchase is excusable, because who wouldn't buy something at a deep discount? Become aware of your bargain-hunting mindset.

My spending rule is quite simple: A bargain isn't a bargain if you don't actually need the item.

There may be a perceived value, but if you're spending money because an item is on sale or discounted, you're not spending on what matters. You're spending on impulse. There is a financial benefit in buying goods that are on sale as long as they are things that have been identified as needed or valued.

Action

Think about your most recent purchases. Identify one purchase you made based solely on its perceived value as a bargain, as opposed to its being needed or wanted. How are you using this item currently?

Know the Difference between Needs and Wants

There's a lot of confusion about the difference between needs and wants. A *need* is something that's required in order for you to live, whereas a *want* is something you might like to have but isn't a necessity. Needs are associated with expenses such as shelter, food, clothing, and medicine.

Transportation to and from work (which is often associated with owning a car) is a need, but options other than a car may be available: for example, carpooling, biking, or public transportation. These options fulfill the *need* for transportation, making the ownership of a car a *want*. It is okay to want a car as long as you're aware of how it serves your purpose. If you can afford to buy one, then you should take comfort in your ability to do so.

A few years ago a friend stated that he needed a new car that could be used to tow his boat from his driveway to the dock at the marina. He'd determined that he needed an SUV but wanted some additional features. He took his time doing some online research in order to find the best SUV in his budget. Once he got to the dealership, the car salesman convinced him to test drive a used but higher-priced Lincoln Navigator. He came to the dealership with a *need* for an SUV and left with a *want* for the Navigator. He didn't make the purchase that day. But, I began noticing a change in his statements about finding an SUV. He stopped saying he needed an SUV and began stating he needed a Lincoln Navigator.

A person's money mindset can blur the line between needs and wants, making it difficult to differentiate between desire and necessity. It may be easy to prioritize the need for food over the need for a new pair of shoes. It does get trickier when you're trying to differentiate between the need for a car and the want for a luxury brand. This is when it becomes important to be clear about your vision and guiding principles so that you can make the best financial decisions.

Let's take, for example, the necessity of functioning in society and being connected through smartphones. You begin by stating that you need a new smartphone, but you want the iPhone. Any smartphone would serve your needs, but a belief that the iPhone is a cooler and better product creates a want. If you continue thinking about the iPhone in this way, you'll find soon enough that you no longer need a smartphone—you need an iPhone. If you remain in your unaware state, you may even convince yourself that you need the more expensive, larger version of the iPhone.

Of course, you can spend your money any way you choose, but your spending should be based on purposeful planning so that you can afford the needs and save for the wants.

Know about Credit as a Financial Tool

On the road to financial wellness, think of credit as a tool (like your car's spare tire) that's helpful when used at the right time and for the right reasons. If the tool is used incorrectly or for long periods of time, it can cause damage.

When I traveled around the world, I realized why so many of us in the United States have been able to improve our lives while many others who live in different countries can't. We have access to credit such as credit cards, personal loans, and lines of credit that is based mostly on personal guarantees of a promise to pay as opposed to being tied to assets.

"You're American. You're so lucky. It's the land of opportunity," said a man from Dalla, Myanmar.

His statement captured what I experienced in many parts of Southeast Asia and Central America. Access to credit has allowed people in the United States the opportunity to own homes, buy cars, and pay college tuition. Because of credit, we have been able to get educated, find good jobs, and move to better neighborhoods.

It was this access to credit that allowed me to invest in my future. I was able to attend college because of student loans. I got a loan to buy a car that helped me get to and from work. In many ways, it was credit that allowed me to get a better job and improve my financial situation.

Credit, I've come to believe, is a tool that, when used mindfully, can help you achieve life milestones that can improve your financial well-being. However, many people use credit for mindless purchases. When you use credit to finance a purchase, you do not own that purchase—you're indebted to it.

"I just bought a living- and dining-room set," said a friend, who had recently moved into a new apartment.

He felt obliged to let me know about the financing terms. "I got a great deal with zero-percent financing for 18 months with the store's credit card," he reported.

"How long is your lease?" I asked.

"It's for a year," he replied.

My friend moved out of the apartment within the year and sold or gave away his furniture. It took him an additional 12 months to pay off the furniture he no longer owned. His total cost was roughly $1,800, while the original price tag was $1,300. Imagine being indebted to your living room furniture like this.

When you don't have enough money, you might rely on credit. Credit isn't the problem per se—but credit used mindlessly leads to debt, shackling you to a purchase that may have far outlived its useful purpose.

Remember that credit is a financial tool that can help you achieve goals.

Know the Power of Time

We have time to complain about our incomes but no time to improve our skill sets. We have time to spend on YouTube but no time to do a budget. We have time for morning coffee runs but can't find the time to review financial statements.

"I don't have time" is a popular excuse given by many people who are convinced they are unable to do something they really want to do. You allocate time to something that's important to you, but you need to be aware of that activity's actual value. In life, if you're aware of what is truly valuable to you, you're mindful about allocating time to it.

Time is the most valuable asset you own, and you get to determine its value. When you're aware of the value of your time, you will make sure to invest it wisely, not spend it mindlessly. Time is finite. Once spent, there is no way for you to make more of it. Yet we find ourselves spending our time on things that do not matter.

Time, like money, is a *resource*. It must be managed. If you make money work for you, you're managing your time effectively. If, however, you are working for money in exchange for your time, you may find yourself running out of time.

The most conventional method of getting money is to exchange our time at work for a paycheck. This practice has caused us to value our time based on the size of our salaries. These salaries are then used to make purchases to pay for our needs and wants. However, if you're exchanging time for money and don't particularly enjoy what you're doing, you may find yourself spending money to comfort yourself for time wasted—creating a vicious cycle.

Remember, what you spend on and how you spend money says a lot about your values and priorities. If you find yourself buying things that do not add value in your life, you're wasting your time.

Do you live opulently or frugally? Luxuriously or creatively?

Just because you find yourself living with the bare essentials doesn't mean you're poor. It could mean you've spent your time on experiences rather than on accumulating things. Or it could be the other way around—perhaps your life can be summed up by the things you own. Be mindful that you're ultimately the judge of how you live. If you realize that you've exchanged your time for things that do not matter to you, you need to make some changes.

Know the power of time when it comes to saving and borrowing—*time can work for you or work against you*. It has the power to increase the value of your savings or decrease the value of your earnings. The money you have today is definitely worth more in the future if saved and invested, a concept often referred to as the *time value of money*. In contrast, the money you borrow—via credit cards and loans—is worth less to you, as you're obligated to pay interest, fees, or both. The longer the time frame for your loan, the more money it will cost you. Be mindful that debt is reserving your future time for work rather than fun. If you want to own your time, avoid debt.

How you choose to spend your time is one of the most important decisions you'll ever make. Don't waste your time. Stop spending time finding reasons something is impossible to accomplish; instead, spend your time figuring out how to make it happen. Your awareness of your time is as important, if not more important, than your awareness of your money beliefs.

If this is truly the only life you have to live, let's make sure it's one in which time was spent consciously on building and living the life you love. Manage time as you manage money. Make the best use of both to spend on things that matter.

 Action

When you're at home, stand at the doorway of a room. Take a look at the things you own. Think of these items in terms of time, not money, spent. For example, if your TV was purchased for $600 and you make $10 per hour, that TV represents 60 hours of your life. The items you have in that room reflect time you're spending. Do they reflect you correctly?

Know Your Financial Numbers

There's a lot of importance placed on credit scores, but that number only indicates how you handle money that was lent to you. The focus on credit scores reflects our society's current obsession with spending and using credit to do so. Your credit score is part of a series of financial numbers you should know, but it isn't the most important number in your financial life. On your road to financial wellness, gain a better understanding of your financial well-being by knowing your credit score, net worth, cash flow, and retirement age.

Credit Score

There's a lot of misinformation that persists about credit. I could write an entire book on this subject; however, I'll focus my attention on the importance of knowing your credit score. I'll start with a brief explanation of credit reports.

A credit report includes personal information and a history of credit use. It includes the credit or loans you've held or have outstanding, the balances and limits for your credit cards, your payment history, credit inquiries, and any public judgments or records. It is from this information that your credit score is generated.

Your credit score is calculated by a credit reporting agency and is based on a variety of factors that come from different organizations. Your credit score can and will vary depending on the credit reporting agency doing the calculating. What is more important is to know where you fall within the credit score range. There are different scoring methodologies and ranges, but a simple search online can help you determine what those methods and score ranges are.

A credit score can impact your ability to obtain additional credit, but as I've stated throughout the book, *credit is a tool*. Credit can help you along the road to financial wellness, or it can derail your efforts to reach your destination. A higher credit score will help you get more favorable credit terms with lower interest rates and lower payments. It's important to manage your credit wisely so that you remain an ideal applicant when you're seeking a mortgage, refinancing a student loan, or applying for a debt-consolidation loan.

Verify the information found in your credit report. Make sure the information found in your credit report is accurate. You can request a free copy of your credit report from the three major credit reporting agencies—Experian, Equifax, and TransUnion—through AnnualCreditReport.com. This is the only government-mandated and authorized website for requesting your free copy of your credit report, which you can do once every 12 months. Review your credit report information and verify its accuracy. If you find a discrepancy or an error, correct the issue directly with the credit reporting agency in question.

You will not get a credit score through AnnualCreditReport.com. To obtain your credit score you must request it from one of the credit reporting agencies and pay a fee. However, a growing number of banks, credit card companies, credit unions, and apps offer access to free credit scores.

I won't go into many more specifics about credit scores, aside from stressing the importance of knowing your score and what it represents: It is an indicator of your credit health. It does not tell you much of anything else.

Action

Request your credit report from AnnualCreditReport.com and ask your financial institutions about accessing free credit scores.

Your Net Worth

Your net worth is an overlooked—yet important—figure to know. Knowing your net worth not only helps you to see where you are today, but it also helps you to envision where you want to be. Your net worth is a snapshot that enables you to easily determine what area of your finances must take priority: paying down debt, increasing savings, cutting expenses, or investing in appreciating assets.

Your net worth helps you understand your financial wealth at a specific point in time. It is the amount by which your assets exceed your liabilities—the difference between what you own and what you owe. Things you own that have value could be your savings and investments, your home, and your car—and anything else that can be sold for a price. Liabilities are things you owe, such as mortgages, loans, and any other type of debt.

Net Worth = What You Own (Assets) − What You Owe (Liabilities)

If the total value of what you own exceeds the total value of what you owe, then you have a positive net worth. You're financially healthy. This number helps you determine if you're on track with your financial wellness or need to make adjustments. If you have a negative net worth it doesn't necessarily mean you're financially unhealthy, but you do owe more than you own. Knowing this should increase your awareness about increasing your assets or lowering your liabilities.

Track your net worth over time. It will help you to see your progress and to remain mindful about what needs to be done to continue on your road to financial wellness.

 Action

Calculate your net-worth number.

Liquid Assets

How much do you have available in case of emergencies? Liquid assets are cash or assets that can easily be converted to cash without substantial penalties or fees. Liquid assets could be cash in the bank or stocks, but your retirement funds are not liquid assets.

Think of your liquid assets as an easily accessible safety net—a spare tire—on the road to financial wellness. It's a tool that can help you through difficult financial periods without impacting your long-term investment strategy. If too much of your assets is in real estate or business ventures, which are more difficult to convert to cash, you may be ill equipped to weather a financial setback if it happens.

Calculate how much you have in available savings—including cash, emergency funds, CDs (certificates of deposit), money markets, stocks in your brokerage accounts, and other assets you can access if an emergency or an unplanned investment opportunity arises.

Knowing your total liquid assets can help you plan a diversified savings and investment strategy that takes into account your changing life and financial situations. If you discover you do not have much in terms of liquid assets, then you may want to budget to build up your emergency fund or keep more of your cash in accessible accounts.

It's recommended that you have at least six months of expenses saved in an emergency fund. Depending on other factors, you may want additional available cash to take advantage of business or investment opportunities that may arise. The amount of liquid assets you'll need for those opportunities may vary. This is an important strategy to ensure financial well-being.

 Action

Determine your liquid-asset number from your net worth.

Cash Flow

Experts often say to live within your means. Some people may even use this principle to chastise others who are in debt for not living within their means. But what does this phrase actually mean?

Are you living paycheck to paycheck? Do you have extra cash on hand after all your expenses are paid? Understanding your cash flow will help you to figure out if you're living within your means. Your cash flow won't tell you when you can retire; however, it can tell you if you're on the right path. Cash flow is how much money is coming in and how much is going out. Analyzing it will reveal surpluses and deficits, and you can use this information to create the necessary strategies to improve your financial wealth.

As you figure out your cash flow, the process may seem similar to creating a budget; however, you won't be too concerned with the total savings or the total debt you have. Instead, you'll just be mindful of the flow of income and expenses within a given period of time—in this case, a month.

To calculate your cash flow, you'll need to gather your total net income from all sources and your total expenses for the month. Count income from all sources that provide you with money to spend (for example, your paycheck, interest income, and investment income). Expenses should include all payments occurring regularly and irregularly (such as your mortgage or rent, car payments, groceries, utilities, and spending money).

Cash Flow = Total Monthly Net Income − Total Monthly Expenses

Having a positive cash flow means you're spending less than you earn, and that surplus can be used to save, invest, and pay off debt. On the other hand, if you have a negative cash flow, it means you're living beyond your means. This can lead to increased credit use and debt. The result of this calculation can help you determine which course of action to take, including cutting expenses, increasing income, and prioritizing debt repayment. It's important to know your cash flow on a monthly basis because this is a more reliable number to determine what you can afford and how much you can spend. This is the true indicator of your means.

 Action

Calculate your cash-flow number.

Retirement Age

I can't wait to retire.

I've said this quite often and previously believed it would be at an age that was decades away. I thought about retirement, but I wasn't mindfully planning for it. I grew up believing that we work as much as we can until the date our bodies are physically unable to because of old age—which also happens to be the time in our lives when we have plenty of free time. Many of us see retirement as that ideal period when we get to have fun and do all the things we've dreamed about—freely able to check off items on our bucket list—and I saw it the same way.

That was until I realized I could retire sooner rather than later. Your retirement age can vary, and it doesn't need to be dictated by your employer or the government. Retirement isn't just an age in our 70s but a lifestyle. Retirement is a state of living in which your income to pay for living expenses doesn't come from the time-for-money work exchange. A state in which you have enough in savings or income-generating investments to cover your living expenses. This income allows you to use your time to pursue work, hobbies, and interests that matter to you.

With effective planning, retirement can happen at any age—or even multiple times in your lifetime. I consider myself retired from my previous career, and I lived for two years solely on my savings.

By 2011 I had been able to save around $35,000, which I used to backpack around the world and pay for living expenses from 2012 to 2014. My expenses at the time were quite low, and I made sure not to spend mindlessly. Everything I purchased had a purpose, and I was mindful to not take on additional expenses that required fixed monthly payments.

For example, if your fixed monthly expenses are $1,500 per month, it would require $18,000 in savings to afford your current lifestyle for a year ($1,500 × 12 months). If you save $18,000 and stay within a $1,500-per-month budget, then you would be able to afford to live without a job for one year. That would give you time to pursue more purposeful work within that time frame. However, spending above your budget would decrease the number of months you'd get to work on your chosen projects.

Set a date right now for your retirement. Be mindful of the lifestyle you want to live and the importance of consciously saving and spending. Be mindful of lifestyle inflation and your spending habits, which could derail your efforts to retire.

 Action

Calculate your monthly expenses and determine how much you'll need to live a retirement lifestyle for just one year.

Currently I am working on projects I am passionate about that generate income. I earn income through writing and speaking engagements, which is quite different from the paycheck I earned working in financial services. I do consider myself to be living a retirement lifestyle. I describe lifestyle budgeting in further detail in Part III, "Creating a Plan."

PART **III**

Creating a Plan

want you to go back and imagine your road trip of life. You know exactly where you're starting from, and you've increased your knowledge of what lies ahead. You've packed your car with all the necessary tools you'll need to get to your destination. Your compass is pointing west, and that's where you want to be. Sure, you can set off on this road trip using only your knowledge of the routes involved and relying on your compass to guide you. You know you'll get there, but you're not exactly sure when you'll arrive. You know there are some places along the way you want to see, but you're unsure if they'll be on the route you're taking. You'll take the chance and figure it out along the way.

What if there was a better way to go on your road trip? What if you had an actual roadmap? You can argue that a smartphone GPS will do just fine. It may even provide you with points of interest along the way. However, a GPS would only get you from start to finish, and the points of interest it gives you would be based on what other people believe is interesting. This approach doesn't require much effort. Once you've entered your starting point and destination address, you can sit back and listen to the GPS voice guiding you to your destination without any consideration of what actually may be of importance or interest to you along the way.

If this is the only road trip you'll go on in your lifetime, why not make sure you figure out what stops you want to make? Why not have more input into which roads you'll use or the places you want to visit? A roadmap is your plan. It will show you the available roads, but you get to decide which roads to take. It can help you visualize the important stops along the way and the exits you'll need to make. You may find something of unexpected interest, and the roadmap can help you determine the detour you need to take to get there. And when you're lost, you can look at this roadmap to get back on the right path. All of these benefits make this roadmap quite valuable.

Do you know how much you're making and how much you're spending? Are you making choices that reflect your values? Do you know what you're working toward?

On my road trip I had a conversation with Michael, a twenty-something waiter working at a high-end restaurant. Michael had been finding it difficult to find his way.

"I can't think about my future when I'm just barely making it now," said Michael.

"Do you know where your money is going?" I asked.

"Yes," he said, and then laughingly added, "my bills are being paid, but I am just not enjoying myself."

"How are you budgeting? What tools are you using to track your money?" I inquired.

"I know where my money is going. I just don't have enough of it," he responded.

"How do you know where it's going? How are you keeping track?" I pressed him further.

"Well, I don't use anything in particular," he stated.

I stood there questioning how certain Michael was about how he was using his money. I wondered how could he know where it was going if he wasn't tracking where it was going. As the conversation continued, he eventually stated that he checked his bank statements monthly. He used a debit card for most purchases and paid his bills using online bill pay. Michael was focusing on one number: what was left over after bills were paid.

"What's stopping you from having a budget?" I asked.

"To be frank, I know where my money is going, and I don't need to be told I can't enjoy my life," he stated, adding, "I work hard to enjoy what I can afford, and I don't want to limit myself from living my life the way I see fit."

This really isn't a unique conversation. I've had many similar conversations around the country. "I know where my money is going" or "I really don't know where it's all going" are common responses to any questions relating to budgets. However, I've learned that the majority of people do not have an actual budget. They use mental accounting to track their income and expenses. So the numbers are fuzzy at best. Mental accounting is influenced by how you're feeling at that moment. You may assign more value to one thing at a certain time in your life, and then something else another time. This mental calculation causes you to believe one week that you're unable to do what you want and another week that you're living life. What is actually happening isn't living but existing within the confines of a paycheck. It's *existing* paycheck to paycheck.

On the road to financial wellness, this roadmap is (dare I say it) a budget. Although you may have shied away from this word in the past, a budget is a spending plan that prioritizes what's important so you can make progress toward living your vision for your life—your destination. With increased understanding of personal finance and a healthier money mindset—your compass—you'll find yourself ready to take on the challenges ahead. This financial roadmap highlights the goals that are important to you and the path you'll need to take to achieve them. But you're not alone—just as you can use a GPS along with your roadmap, you can use financial experts to help with guidance along the way.

In the first stage of the ACT Process, "Awareness," you learned the importance of having a vision for your life. In the second stage, "Creating a Plan," you'll take what you've learned to create the right spending plan that aligns with your values and prioritizes the goals that support the vision for your life. I'll discuss a budgeting framework called the *YOLO budget* that will allow you to enjoy your money today while progressing toward your financial goals. Your budget isn't about depriving you of everything you want, but rather, focusing your attention on the things that matter to you.

A budget is the single most effective tool for identifying and prioritizing spending. I've stressed the importance of your money mindset, and this remains a key concept in the budgeting process. In this stage of the ACT process, you'll learn about the following:

- ▪ Building a lifestyle budget and spending plan
- ▪ Using the purposeful money strategy to spend and save
- ▪ Improving credit use and eliminating debt forever

CHAPTER 6

Building a Lifestyle Budget and Spending Plan

For years I knew how important it was to have a budget, but I couldn't convince myself to create one. I spent three and a half years at a credit union with millions of dollars in assets, managing the marketing and business-development budget. I knew from a professional standpoint that a budget was a plan to allocate resources to achieve desired results, but I couldn't apply my knowledge to my personal life. Sure, I used a number of budgeting apps and tools that were readily and freely available, but they just reminded me how much of a failure I was with my finances. I saw where I was spending my money, and it did make me wonder what changes I could make—but even all of this information about my spending didn't change any of my financial behaviors. In fact, the more I saw where my money was going—and realized that it was not contributing to my happiness—the more I sought satisfaction through consumption. I understood that a budget was a plan, but I (like many other people) also felt that budgets were personally limiting.

Let's deal with the terminology first. A budget is a plan. It's as simple as that. You want less uncertainty in life? Draft a plan. A budget is your first step in turning a dream into an actual lifestyle. A personal budget is a spending plan that can help you reach milestones and achieve quantifiable financial goals. You prioritize spending on what you need and want, thus reducing waste of resources: your time and money. With the right money mindset and clarity about your values, you can create a spending plan with financial goals that matter to you and a budget that supports the vision for your life. A budget should help you do the following:

- Save and spend your money.
- Focus attention on your priorities.
- Pay yourself first.
- Repay debt and loan obligations.
- Reduce expenses.
- Increase income.
- Live your dream lifestyle.

Budgets, however, still make people cringe. During my events around the country, I've seen many people nod in agreement whenever I mention the importance of a budget. However, when I've asked people to raise their hands to show how many actually have a budget, I find that only a few do. And the types of budgets range from ones with actual details to those consisting of mental budgeting.

You might find yourself avoiding the "b" word too. You might associate the word "budget" with limitation and deprivation. In many cases, including my own, the idea of a budget brought fears of lifestyle changes. I was used to living in a certain way, good or not, and I didn't want to disrupt what I was used to. If a budget might show that I didn't have enough money and force me to come face-to-face with my bad financial decisions, I would avoid it at all costs—even if that meant not living the life of my dreams. I preferred to keep my head buried in the sand.

My aha budgeting moment occurred when I began to question my morning coffee-and-bagel routine. If I didn't know where my money was going, how effective could I be in cultivating my dream lifestyle? As I became clearer in seeing and understanding my values, I was forced into a deeper financial awareness. If a plan to spend tens of thousands of dollars could lead to company growth, then what was stopping me from spending my tens of thousands of dollars to achieve my own personal growth? A personal budget was the answer.

I've had these personal budget conversations with family and friends. I recall one particular conversation with my friend Michael after I asked him to come meet me for dinner.

"I can't go to dinner. I'm on a budget," Michael said.

I took his response as an opportunity to understand how he was using the word *budget*.

"Is dinner with a friend something you'd enjoy?" I asked.

"Of course, it's always a good time. But I'm on a budget, so I can't go tonight," he responded.

Michael and I met for dinner (on me), and we had a lengthy conversation about money. I realized a behavioral pattern in my friend that I hadn't noticed until we had this discussion, and I asked him directly if I could look at his budget. Michael confessed that he has never had an *actual* budget.

Michael found himself saying repeatedly that he was on a budget, preventing him from freely doing things he enjoyed. After paying his bills on payday, Michael would see if he had any money left over to do what he wanted to, such as having dinner with friends that weekend. Michael's idea of budgeting was not budgeting. Michael was using mental accounting and an approach of just getting by to manage his money. If it was a week without a payday, he'd tell his friends he was on a budget. He said it was liberating when he had extra money on a payday, but that during the weeks when he did not, his life was quite stressful. That's not living—it's just *existing*. Michael was existing paycheck to paycheck and using his payday to determine what he could or could not do.

After our conversation, Michael realized he was using the word budget incorrectly. And he's not alone. I've met many others around the country like him, in different walks of life—from people making minimum wage to those making six-figure salaries—who use mental accounting and paydays as their budgets. I was once part of this group.

"I can't make it to that weekend trip," I once said, adding, "I just don't have the money in my budget." I didn't actually have a budget at the time, so what I was really saying was this: I don't know if I will have any money left over after this paycheck to pay for the cabin and meals.

During that period of my life I didn't have a plan for the things I wanted to do. I was only choosing to do them if money was left over from my paycheck or I could put the expense on a credit card. I had absolutely no desire to have a budget. I didn't want to spend time planning a route when I didn't even know where I was going. My thinking back then was: I can't do all the things I want, but at least I'm doing some of them.

DEALING WITH YOUR FEAR OF LIFESTYLE CHANGE

I once had a discussion about fear with my brother John, who is a board-certified behavioral analyst.

"We're creatures of habit," he stated, "and we're willing to continue to do things that aren't really good for us. It's not because we want it, but it's what we're used to. Any changes to what we're used to can create fear and anxiety because of uncertainty."

The uncertainty of how we'll feel after a change is so profound that we would rather not go through any process that supports change. We take comfort in what we currently know or don't know.

So what stopped Michael and me from budgeting? We both feared a change in our lifestyles. It was fear that enabled me to continue just existing from paycheck to paycheck. I was working really hard for money, and at times I was able to do what I wanted. I wasn't forced to make any changes, so I didn't make any. My fear of changing a lifestyle that I was used to scared me into inaction.

"We have to make changes when we're confronted with the facts," my brother said.

In cases where we fear a lifestyle change, we'll do nothing unless we absolutely must. We'll avoid the budgeting process so we don't have to make changes.

As my finances deteriorated, having leftover money became less frequent, and as my credit card limits were reached, I faced a dilemma. My lifestyle was leveraged, and I could not exchange any more time to make more money. I was being forced to change, and I needed to regain control. Although it had been some time since I'd attended a budgeting class, the old lessons resurfaced. A budget was going to be the tool I used to improve my situation. However, I had to think of budgeting differently. My budget had to be a *plan* that empowered me to afford those weekend trips and at the same time progress toward life and financial goals.

The stages of awareness I went through started with the money mindset that had formed my financial behaviors and habits. When I became mentally and emotionally clear about my values, I was able to envision my dream lifestyle. That vision for my life helped me identify the financial goals I needed to support the lifestyle I wanted. At that point I just needed a plan to achieve those financial goals, and my budget was going to be part of that plan.

There are many reasons that the majority of people do not have a budget. It takes time to create one and energy to follow through with it. And it's always easier to do nothing than it is to do something. The mindset that may be keeping you from creating your spending plan may include one, a combination, or all of the following elements:

- **A budget is a reminder of past mistakes.** You don't want to confront the bad financial decisions you've made, because doing so causes grief. A budget is going to make you come face-to-face with your zero-balance savings account and spotlight your insurmountable debt. You may also need to confront the reality that your financial decisions led to the life you're currently living, and that it's a life that you don't enjoy. Your financial mistakes must be acknowledged, because this increased awareness of them will improve your decision making in the future.

- **You're afraid you'll realize there is not enough money.** You want to avoid anxiety after realizing the lifestyle you're living isn't affordable or sustainable. This is part of the "fear of lifestyle change." You choose to remain unaware because "ignorance is bliss." However, if you don't know what you have to work with, then it's harder to make decisions to improve your situation. If you're still spending on things that don't matter, then you're wasting your money, and there won't be enough for the things that do matter.

■ **You believe budgeting is unnecessary.** You aren't in a financial bind, and you're saving money. You believe a budget won't
be effective in your situation, because you're handling money
quite well. Or you've tried having a budget in the past, and it
just didn't work out. You might even believe you make way
too much money to be lost in the details such that "budgets
are things people without means have." Budgets are necessary
regardless of the income you make. A budget will help you prioritize your goals and make money work for you.

What's keeping you from having a budget? Your answer to this
question may be different from any that I've just discussed. If you're
finding yourself unable to plan for the life of your dreams, you will still
need to grow your awareness and change your mindset.

The right budget is a plan that helps you to reach goals and limit
uncertainty. Remember, a budget is your spending plan to achieve a
desired outcome; in creating it, you're thinking about how the future
can be and the things you want in that future. As you become aware
of what is important to you, you'll find that the fear you had about
changes to your lifestyle is unfounded. You'll see that there will be less
back-and-forth happening in your mind and less what-if thinking about
missed opportunities. You'll find it easier to say yes to the things that
add value in your life and no to things that don't matter (without guilt).

A budget is your plan, and budgeting is the process you'll use to
create your plan. There are many tools available to assist you in the
budgeting process—from your parents' spreadsheet or paper method
to using software and apps to quantify your spending. The key is to
find the tool that works for you. The process of budgeting is meant to
identify your actual expenses and spending habits, and you need a tool
that does that. It should help you identify specific changes that need to
be made—the more details the better, because your goal is to shape a
budget that's more reflective of the lifestyle you want.

I originally used a shoebox for my budgeting process. I gathered
all of my pay stubs, receipts, statements, and bills for an entire month
and placed all of them into a shoebox. A few days into the following
month, I took out the shoebox and began categorizing my expenses:
for example, housing, transportation, food, entertainment, and other
categories. I now had a pile of papers on the floor. I used a notebook to

write down the types and amounts of my income and expenses. This was the first time I'd ever had a clear picture of my money and how I was spending it. I used this information to create my budget. It was an effective start that helped me visualize my finance situation and feel the impact of my spending on it, but eventually I began using a mobile app to help me track expenses.

You can use my shoebox method or you can use any of a number of available apps that can track your spending and allow you to categorize it. Choose the method that you feel most comfortable with, and choose a different method if your first choice doesn't work out.

Now that you have your income and expenses set up, you might be wondering what follows. The traditional next step advocated by financial gurus has been to use whatever rule they deem to represent the most appropriate way to spend and allocate your money. Based on the information you've gathered about your spending and expenses, you are then asked to make changes to your expenses and to curb your spending to reflect one of the following budget frameworks:

- **60 percent rule.** This budget allocates 60 percent of your income for monthly expenses, defined as housing, utilities, food, transportation, and other fixed payments. Thirty percent of your income goes toward financial goals; specifically, 10 percent toward retirement, 10 percent toward short-term savings, and 10 percent toward debt reduction. The remaining 10 percent is used for spending.

- **70-20-10 rule.** This budget allocates 70 percent of your income toward living expenses, defined as all monthly expenses—from housing and transportation to discretionary spending. The next 20 percent of your income goes toward your savings goals; specifically, 10 percent for retirement, 5 percent for an emergency fund, and 5 percent on other specific goals. If you have debt, the remaining 10 percent is for paying it off.

- **50-30-20 rule.** This budget allows you to spend more freely, with 30 percent of your income allocated toward personal spending, such as concerts and clothing. The majority of your income (50 percent) is for fixed expenses, such as housing and transportation. The remaining 20 percent goes toward financial goals, such as saving for retirement and paying off debt.

Although these rules can be useful budget frameworks, it's these types of approaches that often can take you off your road to financial wellness. It's assumed that you're the same as others, so the budgets do not reflect your values or your goals. For example, you may be living a frugal lifestyle, in which case spending 60 percent of your salary on monthly expenses seems excessive. You most likely could save half of that allocation toward your early retirement plans.

Also, budget rules that depend on fixed percentages might suggest not spending more than 5 percent of your salary on entertainment and vacations. However, you may want to live an adventure-filled lifestyle. Instead of allocating 50 percent of your income to housing and transportation expenses, you could allocate 25 percent of income toward your adventures.

My experience using these kinds of budgeting methods and my growing awareness of my values and my vision for my life led me to create a more realistic budgeting framework that supported my living my dream lifestyle in this lifetime. This framework merges the YOLO mindset with a budgeting method that takes into account both a person's beliefs and his or her values.

It's your life. If you only live once, don't let me or anyone else stop you from living the life of your dreams on your own terms.

LIVING THE YOLO LIFESTYLE

I remember the period of my life when I wanted a BMW. I ended up owning two of them in my lifetime. I once dreamed of going around the world. Years later, I was backpacking through 20 countries in one year.

I often used to say that since I'll only live once, I'll do as I please—but that thinking led to some decisions not beneficial to my well-being. YOLO was my reason to do crazy things and go on mindless spending sprees. YOLO thinking without the right money mindset subjected me to a number of financial twists and turns. With the right mindset, however, I was able to make financial decisions that supported my vision for my life and achieving my goals in this lifetime. It took me a number of years to finally understand what living YOLO truly meant. Living YOLO isn't living carelessly. It means mindfulness in creating a life worth living. Being strapped to a desk, working nine to five every Monday through Friday, unable to do things that uplifted my heart and soul, meant I wasn't living life—I was just existing, and every purchase I made was to cope with a life of mere existence.

I could say that you need to sacrifice everything now in order to live your dreams tomorrow. But that's not the YOLO mindset I've been talking about. If you only live once, today is as good as any day to live the life of your dreams. As you become more aware of your mindset, gain clarity about your values, and have a vision for your life, you need a plan to get to your destination. However, life isn't just about where you began and what happens at the end. It's about how and what you're doing in between.

I've had many conversations with friends about financial decisions made in the moment that were against their better judgment, given all the facts available. If your desire to live in the moment outweighs your vision for your life, then there's incompatibility between the lifestyle you've chosen and what you say is your dream lifestyle. I had one such conversation with my friend Kelly.

"You're so lucky," Kelly said.

I responded with confusion, "What makes me so lucky?"

"You've been all over the world. You're traveling to places I've only dreamed of, and here I am working every day," she continued.

"That doesn't make me lucky. I have my priorities, and right now it's traveling," I countered.

"Well, I can't do what you're doing. I have so many bills," she responded. "I can't just get up one day and leave my job. You're lucky you were able to do that."

"It wasn't luck," I reiterated.

"You made a lot more money than me. I'm just saying you're luckier, that's all," she said.

I moved toward the window and stared out onto the street.

"It must be nice driving a new Mercedes-Benz," I replied, pointing out the window.

At that time, I no longer owned a car. I had sold my car and was using public transportation and car-sharing apps to get to wherever I wanted to go. The minor inconvenience of not having my own car was offset by the thousands of dollars a year I saved on car payments, insurance premiums, maintenance, and registration fees. Those savings were being used to do more of the things I wanted to—such as travel.

"I work hard," my friend said defensively.

"I have no question that you work really hard, but are you working for the right reasons?" I asked.

"I work hard to live a nice life," she replied.

My friend and I continued the conversation, and what I uncovered isn't at all uncommon. I, too, have used exactly the same reasoning for the lifestyle choices I made. I worked really hard and made really good money, but I was using that money to live a lifestyle that didn't represent my values. I, too, once owned a luxury car so I could live a nice life, yet I dreamed for a lifestyle of freedom.

"What do you want to achieve?" I continued to ask.

"I want to have financial freedom," she responded.

"What does financial freedom mean to you?" I questioned.

My friend stared at me and then turned her gaze away. She looked like she was in deep thought.

"I just want to be able to buy the things I want so I can live my dream. Having more money is going to help me accomplish that," she eventually said.

At this point, I clarified that buying things wasn't going to create her dream lifestyle. Money should not be the end goal—it should be used to create more opportunities to build the ideal life. I define financial freedom as living life on my terms without thought of money or finances. It's living a lifestyle devoid of the anxiety of having too little or too much money. It's having the mindset that I control money, which I use as a tool, not as an end goal. This is the only life I have to live, and financial freedom means I have more opportunity to use my time for things that matter and to fill my years with purpose.

My friend's belief that she could spend her way to a meaningful life was based on her scarcity mindset. If you want more money so you can buy that larger home, then you'll also have a larger mortgage payment. If you need a bigger salary to afford the luxury car, then you'll also have a bigger car payment. Your money mindset shouldn't be about increasing your ability to spend more, but rather about having the opportunity to build a rich and purposeful life.

I've talked to many financially independent people and extremely wealthy individuals. These people do not think of money the way many of us think of money. Money isn't a means to an end. Money is a resource to be invested.

There is absolutely nothing wrong with owning a luxury car, or living in a better neighborhood, or spending your years traveling around the world. However, if you're making specific spending decisions to cope with a lifestyle you don't enjoy, it's time to make new choices.

It's time to define what *living once* means to you.

What is your definition of financial freedom?

After you've answered this question, you'll want to continue to clarify *your definition* of financial freedom. Now, ask yourself these follow up questions:

- What does freedom, in general, mean in my life?
- What do I hope to be doing when I've reached a state of financial freedom?
- Does financial freedom mean an increased capacity to buy more?
- What financial situation do I believe is keeping me from having financial freedom right now?

THE YOLO BUDGET

As stated earlier, most personal finance books focus on identifying your financial goals and then providing a plan to achieve them. In this book, I've used a great deal of time to talk to you about your mindset and dreams. I can't reiterate enough the importance of cultivating a healthy money mindset, because it will change how you work toward your dreams. But dreams can only manifest if you have a plan to achieve them.

The YOLO budget is a framework for building your plan and helping you enjoy your money today, while still progressing toward your financial goals. It combines everything I've talked about: your mindset, your awareness of your values, and your vision for your life. You're now at the point at which you need to create the plan that allows you to live your life today while making progress toward your vision.

If you only live once, why not spend it doing things you enjoy most of the time, rather than just some of the time? YOLO means using your money in the way that most effectively maximizes your enjoyment.

During my road trip I had a conversation with a personal-finance blogger. At one point in her life she, too, had lived a YOLO lifestyle.

"YOLO? Isn't that a bad motto when it comes to spending?" asked the blogger.

"It certainly has been used to excuse spending mindlessly, but I use YOLO in a new context. If this is indeed the only life we have to live, then we should make it as enjoyable as possible," I replied.

"That's reckless. You're telling people to spend on whatever it is they want," she continued.

"You're absolutely right. There's no purpose in spending my hard-earned money on what other people want. It should be what I want," I said.

"You're steering people the wrong way," she stated.

I had to disagree, because telling people what they should be doing with money has been the problem all along. We can continue to force people into boxes and conformity, but that has only led to our society's obsession with consumerism and mindless consumption. We all have the opportunity to define what *living once* means, and with the right money mindset and a budget framework we'll live a far better life working toward our own goals instead of stressing over goals that were set by others.

I continued the conversation with the personal-finance blogger, offering my experience.

"That's the beauty of the YOLO budget. It takes into consideration your time and values and how you choose to define your life," I stated and then asked, "Why should I tell someone he must own a home? Why should I tell someone that her retirement should be planned like everyone else's?"

Maybe you feel exactly the same way as the blogger. Or maybe you've come to understand that this is, in fact, your life, and the lifestyle you're living is a result of your decisions. You have the power to make choices more reflective of your values. That is the essence of the YOLO budget.

On your road to financial wellness, you need a roadmap with the routes and pit stops that will take you on the most enjoyable path to your destination. While most of budgeting is tedious and boring, I want you to think of the YOLO budget as empowering and liberating. This budget framework is an effective tool to build a plan aligned with your values. Remember: Some things matter, but not all things matter.

My money philosophy: There isn't enough time and money for everything, but there could be enough for some things. Know what the *some things* are.

The YOLO budget is the framework that gets you from where you are today to where you want to be tomorrow. It will help you identify and prioritize the things that matter to you. Your budget should support living your dream lifestyle in this lifetime. And you can create that lifestyle with the right spending plan. As you go through the YOLO budget framework, here are a few things I want you to keep in mind:

- Remain mindful of your values and vision for your life.
- Be specific about your goals and think success.
- Stay organized and remain realistic.
- Track everything and keep in control.
- Monitor progress and expect setbacks along the way.
- Reward yourself for reaching milestones.
- Make it easy and simple.
- Use free tools and resources.
- Continue to grow your financial awareness.

Use YOLO as a guiding principle in this budgeting process. When you're mindful of the vision for your life because you recognize you only live once, you might be surprised to find that your vision doesn't include owning a home, driving a luxury car, or traveling. It might be much simpler. YOLO is about time and using your time to do more of the things that matter, which might include more time to spend with family, friends, and hobbies.

With the YOLO budget, your budget will vary from those of others because you're planning for your life and not re-creating theirs. This budget will help you plan to live life on your terms. There are no specific spending percentages to use; however, you can use any of the percentage frameworks I've discussed in conjunction with this budgeting process. Remember, your main objective is to identify how you want to live and what you want to achieve and prioritize your spending on those areas.

Every budget framework takes time to complete, but the payoff is tremendous. The YOLO budget is going to help you create the spending plan that's reflective of your desired lifestyle. This framework is a simple way to increase your financial awareness and to help you spend money while still progressing toward goals. You've already learned to have a vision for your life and gained clarity about your values. Now I'll take you through the framework to make mindful lifestyle choices and create your plan. There are six steps in the YOLO budgeting process:

1. Take a step back.
2. Envision your dream lifestyle.
3. Set financial goals.
4. Calculate the numbers.
5. Allocate your money.
6. Monitor and adjust accordingly.

I'll be covering each of these steps in the following sections.

Step 1: Take a Step Back

I'd accepted where I was starting from, and I had a bold vision for the future. However, I still needed to remain mindful of the present. It's great to be working toward something, but if you're not seeing progress toward that vision, it becomes harder to proceed. That's why many of us, even with a vision, get derailed. We take wrong turns and make the wrong decisions. And we find ourselves back where we started. Then we tell ourselves we were foolish for thinking that we could live the life we've dreamed of.

Let's think of budgets as life instruction manuals. They are the detailed instructions that you must follow in order to construct the life you have a vision of. Right now you have a clear picture of what you need to build, and you have all the parts necessary laid out on the floor. In one hand you have your hammer, and in the other you have your manual. You have an idea of how to build your structure and are confident in your ability to figure it out. Which do you now choose? Toss the manual aside and bang away with the hammer, or use the manual to guide you? There is a correct answer. If you choose the latter you'll be choosing the easier route, one with less wasted time and energy. Accept the budget as your manual.

Reflect back on all that you've learned, and remain mindful of your values and the vision for your life when proceeding with the next steps. Earlier I discussed the importance of knowing your net-worth and cash-flow numbers as part of your financial awareness. Know your true income and how it's spent with pinpoint accuracy. Get more specific about your financial situation to identify your financial goals.

With my old job I was able to pay for monthly expenses and periodically had extra money to spend as I wished. Unfortunately I didn't consider my positive cash flow as an opportunity to improve my well-being. When financial times became tougher, knowing my cash-flow number would have placed a spotlight on my spending problem sooner. I could have created strategies to increase income and reduce expenses to get back to a positive cash flow.

The same was true of my net worth. I didn't know about my big financial picture. Although I made a good salary and could cover my monthly expenses, my negative net worth would have indicated I couldn't afford a financial setback. I had more liabilities than assets. If I had been aware of my net-worth number, I would have made different choices to increase my wealth. However, as it stood then, my net worth indicated I needed to continue to work indefinitely.

Your cash flow and net worth are indicators of your financial well-being and your capability to achieve wealth. Your cash-flow number can be affected quicker than your net worth because you can increase income and reduce expenses or alter your spending within a given month. In contrast, it takes a bit more mid- to long-term planning to change your net-worth number. These two numbers are going to be useful as you create your YOLO budget. And you'll gain awareness about how to positively impact these numbers to achieve success.

Cash Flow—Income and Expenses

Cash flow is calculated by subtracting your total monthly expenses from your total net monthly income. Your cash-flow number helps you to determine if you're living within your means. *Living within your means* is defined as the financial capability to pay all your expenses with your income. After calculating your cash flow, you may find that you have a surplus that can be used toward financial goals or spent on unplanned lifestyle experiences.

Use the following formula to calculate your cash-flow number:

Cash Flow = Total Net Monthly Income − Total Monthly Expenses

If you find you have a deficit—meaning your expenses are more than your income—that is an indication that you're living above your means. With a deficit, you either won't be contributing toward your financial goals or you'll be relying on credit to cover the deficit—or both.

With either scenario—positive or negative cash flow—you'll need to craft a strategy that improves your financial situation. A positive cash flow might mean an opportunity to build wealth and invest in other income-generating assets and ventures. A negative cash flow might mean a strategy to cut expenses and eliminate debt to reduce monthly payments.

Net Worth—the Big Financial Picture

Your net worth is an indicator of your wealth. It's the big financial picture and snapshot of your finances at any given point in time. This helps you look at the forest and not just the trees. Your net worth includes all your assets, such as cash in bank accounts, stocks, properties, and business ventures. It also includes all your liabilities, such as your mortgage and other debts. You need to be aware of your net worth because it will help you to determine which financial areas need attention.

Use the following formula to calculate your net-worth number:

Net Worth = Money Owned (Assets) − Money Owed (Liabilities)

If you have a positive net worth, then you could cover all of your liabilities if you cashed in or sold your assets. However, a positive net worth does not mean you can cover your monthly expenses. When you have cash assets, there is a better likelihood that you have funds available to cover emergencies and offset changes in income to pay for monthly expenses. If you have a negative net worth then you are overleveraged, with more outstanding loans than you have assets, and you have no wealth.

Whether you have a positive or negative net worth, there are strategies you can follow to improve your situation. With a negative net worth, you'll need to have financial goals aimed at reducing your loan balances. With a positive net worth, you can determine if you have cash or assets that can easily be converted to cash to pay off liabilities. Decreasing your liabilities can increase your net worth and positively impact your cash flow as well. You can also use cash and invest in income-generating activities to replace your time-for-money paycheck.

Step 2: Envision Your Dream Lifestyle

Your lifestyle choices play a big role in the YOLO budget. You must have a vision for your life to gain clarity about the lifestyle you want to live. Your vision is what you're striving to achieve, while your lifestyle is how you're living. Your vision should be supported by your lifestyle choices, and your lifestyle choices should be supported by financial goals aligned with your values.

I live a number of lifestyles. I have a minimalist lifestyle. I also live an active and adventurous lifestyle. As a minimalist, I do not seek to acquire many possessions. I buy a new pair of shoes when my old pair is completely unusable. As an adventure seeker, I enjoy hiking and traveling. However, contrary to what you might think, I don't live a frugal lifestyle, because I won't sacrifice quality to save a few dollars.

I work on projects that matter to me and take consulting jobs and speaking gigs with companies that are interesting and aligned with my values. This enables me to pay for my living expenses and supports my desire to remain a digital nomad. I can work anywhere in the world. I'm not chasing a paycheck or exchanging my time for money. I'm getting paid for my knowledge and to do only the things that I enjoy. My lifestyles have changed over the years, but I am now more aware of my lifestyle choices and the financial goals that support them.

You might have a similar lifestyle to mine, or you may live with a very different set of lifestyle choices. You may have a single, luxury,

urban, family, or party lifestyle—and you're making financial decisions to support your definition of those lifestyles. If you're not aware
of your lifestyle choices, then you are setting financial goals that can
be in contradiction to your vision—your greater version of you. Get
clear about the lifestyle you're living today, as well as the lifestyle you
actually want to live. Choose the lifestyle that aligns with your values
and helps you progress to your vision.

Let's revisit a question I've asked before: Do you have a vision for
your life?

Now, ask yourself more questions that will clarify the lifestyles that
will support that vision. Ask yourself these questions:

- What lifestyle do I dream of having?
- What lifestyle supports my vision for my life?
- What lifestyle am I currently living?

The wrong lifestyle choices can lead to mindless consumption and
the wrong types of expenses. Let's say, for example, that your vision
is a life of travel, yet you're living a lifestyle of luxury. This lifestyle
causes you to take on debt to finance a larger home and a luxury car.
You're spending money on designer labels and brand names. You're
now required to work more hours to get more money. You complain
that you're unable to travel because you're chronologically and financially limited. Take a step back and have a self-aware view of the lifestyle you're living. In this scenario, are you spending money on the
lifestyle you want?

The answer is no.

There are many people I've met who believe they cannot have a
healthy lifestyle unless they can pay for a gym membership, yet they
live near a county park with miles of running trails. I've also met others who live a party lifestyle but hope to settle down and start a family,
yet make no attempt at dating. You can see the disconnect between
what we say we want and what we actually do.

How can you determine your lifestyle choices?

Your vision can help define the lifestyle you want to live and will
become the benchmark against which you contrast the lifestyle you're
actually living. This is a powerful insight that can only be achieved
through awareness. In addition, what you buy also says a lot about the

lifestyle you're living or the one you want to live. Being mindful with your spending will help you make better lifestyle choices.

A lifestyle choice is subjective; financial goals are objective. It may be easier to set financial goals such as home ownership, owning a car, and traveling around the world because these goals have a price tag, whereas a lifestyle does not have a direct cost. Lifestyle can be made of the places you live, the things you do, and the things you own. So, your lifestyle choices do have an associated cost.

For example, let's say you want to live in a major city and have a financial goal of owning a car. The cost of living in a big city is high, but the opportunities available will support your vision for your life. Would you spend your money on an apartment in a big city to achieve the lifestyle you want? Would you opt to live in a smaller town and own the car you've set as a goal? When you have a vision and clarity about your lifestyle choices, you'll opt for the apartment in the big city and use mass transit instead.

You might find yourself dreaming of a cliffside home overlooking the Pacific Ocean or sailing around the world. The reality may be that your finances cannot support that type of lifestyle at the moment. But you can plan on making it happen. When you're clear about your dream lifestyle and financial goals, you'll create the right plan and make better financial decisions. As you continue to grow in awareness, keep in mind that it isn't about affording everything but affording the right things.

How can you figure out the lifestyles you want to live?

Think about your interests. Choose things you are interested in and contemplate how they relate to your vision for your life. Ask yourself additional questions to gain more clarity:

- What am I interested in doing?
- What do I want to achieve?
- Where do I want to live?

Step 3: Set Financial Goals

With many other types of budgets, you might start with setting financial goals and then review your finances to create a lifestyle you'll enjoy living. The YOLO budget has you prioritize your lifestyle choices over financial goals for a reason. If I started the budgeting process with "What are your goals?" I would receive responses such as "I want to pay off debt" or "I want to buy a home" or "I want a new car."

These responses would be based on someone's perception of how to create a lifestyle. If you haven't gone through the process of understanding your cash flow, your net worth, and your lifestyle goal, you'll continue to set financial goals that are not aligned with your values.

As you continue on your road to financial wellness, your growing awareness of your finances and of the things you value will impact the goals you've created. Along this route, you'll set financial goals and achieve them, or you'll set goals and decide to change them. The more clarity you gain as you practice awareness, the more you'll come to realize that some goals aren't important to you. Your desire for certain goals will evolve through time and it's important to be aware of those changes.

Have you identified any of your financial goals?

Mindful of your lifestyle choices and aware of your financial numbers, you can now identify financial goals, such as starting an emergency fund or paying off student loans or moving to a new city or going back to school. You can ask yourself these questions to get clear on goals you may want to set:

- What are the things I want to accomplish?
- What do I want to experience?
- What do I want to own?

I want you to think about what you want to purchase: goods, experiences, education, and so on. You can relate these purchases to your financial goals in terms of savings needed, debt elimination, college tuition, home ownership, or the vacation of a lifetime.

Keep in mind that financial goals are monetarily quantifiable aspects of your life. Financial goals are specific, reasonable and realistic, and measurable.

Specific. Each goal must be identified with its cost and price point.

Reasonable and realistic. The goal must relate to your vision.

Measurable. The goal should have a time frame and deadline.

There are financial goals such as having an emergency fund, saving for retirement, and eliminating debt that must be prioritized.

These financial goals improve your net worth, build wealth, and secure your future. Take a look at how you can impact your wealth through your net-worth number. If you don't have an emergency fund, then it should be a priority to have one. If you haven't contributed to your company's 401(k), it's time to catch up. If you have debt, use available cash to pay it off sooner. Answer the following questions:

- Which of your assets contribute to your vision for your life, and are they things you want?
- Take a look at your liabilities. What debts do you have that are preventing you from having financial freedom?
- What things do you want to own, and what experiences do you want to have?

Here are some examples of different types of goals:

Types of Goals That Increase Your Wealth

- Building an emergency fund.
- Paying off student loans.
- Paying off credit-card debt.
- Getting your graduate degree or certification.
- Saving for mortgage down payment.
- Saving for retirement.

Type of Goals That Add to Your Lifestyle

- Going on an around-the-world vacation.
- Buying a new laptop.
- Owning a dream car.
- Moving to a new city.
- Having a new DSLR camera.

After you've identified your goals, ask yourself clarifying questions such as these:

- Is this goal aligned with my vision for my life?
- How is this goal supporting my lifestyle choice?
- Does this goal represent what I value?

Get clear on what you absolutely must have. Rely on the growing awareness of what you value and what goals propel you forward in living your vision.

Saving

Saving is a major component of the YOLO budget. You need to incorporate a healthy savings strategy into your budget to ensure you're securing your future. Savings will allow you to handle the unexpected much more confidently. The more you save, the less you'll need to work in the future, and the more free time you'll have to pursue the things that matter to you. The following savings categories will help you identify your financial goals and link them to a corresponding timeline to achieve them:

- **Emergency fund**. Have six months of living expenses available in cash or assets that can easily be converted to cash for emergency situations, such as loss of a job or a medical emergency.
- **Short-term goals.** These are goals for the next 6 to 12 months. They include holiday gift giving, vacations, and big-ticket consumer purchases, such as smartphones, computers, and weekend getaways.
- **Mid-term goals.** These are goals with a time frame of between two and five years. This category includes saving for things such as buying time to find a more rewarding career, having enough for a mortgage down payment, buying a car, getting new equipment for your photography or film hobby, or taking your dream vacation around the world.
- **Long-term goals.** These are goals for the next five years or more. These relate to your retirement goals and purchases of income-generating assets for the time when you no longer work for a paycheck. This category includes contributions to your 401(k), IRAs, stocks, index funds, and insurance as well as investments in businesses and other appreciating assets. This may also include college planning for young families.

Debt

With the YOLO budget, your goal is to remove the debt ball and chain forever, and that means eliminating debt. Prioritize debt repayment based on interest rate and primary purpose of the debt. For example, pay off all credit cards and unsecured debts first. These debts no longer contribute to your life because you're most likely paying for things whose usable value has already been eclipsed. Next, pay off student loans that, for many of us, are the bulk of our debt. And last, begin the process of eliminating your car loan and mortgage.

Remember, when you're paying off debt, the process includes not adding to debt. If you're unable to pay your credit card in full each month, do not continue to use your credit card to make purchases that will add to your debt balance.

You must be exact in specifying the amount you need to save and the amount you need to pay off when setting goals. You need exact numbers in order to allocate your income accordingly.

Prioritizing Goals

As you set your financial goals, you might discover that you have more goals than you have available money. You might even feel overwhelmed. Don't get discouraged. The good thing about the YOLO budget is that while some financial goals are recommended, you're setting the majority of your goals based on what you need and want. Your goals should reflect your financial reality and at the same time be aligned with your values. Prioritize the financial goals that will help you progress toward the vision for your life. Keep these things in mind:

- Use your healthy money mindset and money philosophy to improve your financial behaviors and change your habits.
- Be mindful of what's important in determining which financial goals contribute to the lifestyle you want to live.
- Select financial goals that will expedite reaching your destination.
- Focus on goals that increase your wealth.
- Practice self-awareness to maintain balance between finances and experiences.

Step 4: Calculate the Numbers

In my seminars I talk about the importance of having exact financial numbers. The financial numbers you use to create your budget must be accurate.

"I know exactly how much I have because I get paid this Friday," said a man from the Chicago event, who added, "I know how much I am paying and who I am paying."

In the months after the road trip I built a working relationship with this man, and I helped him through the budgeting process. As we followed the steps in the budgeting process I discovered that his financial numbers were fluctuating: He gave me two different amounts for the rent he paid for his apartment, three different amounts for his car payment, and a very convoluted dollar amount for groceries. It turned out that all of his numbers were estimates. He had been adamant that the numbers were correct when he gave them to me. However, the numbers weren't correct. He was off by $50 on the rent he paid. And he spent way more on groceries than he could have ever imagined. He estimated "around $250 per month," but the amount he spent on groceries was actually closer to $400 per month.

If you don't know your exact numbers, you're not on a budget. You're using mental accounting. Having exact numbers is necessary. You need specific details about your monthly income, expenses, and spending behavior. These details will reveal how much you actually need to live and where you must cut expenses in order to shift your money to the areas that are most important.

This is where the tedious part of budgeting comes in, but it's a part that's integral to the framework. It will increase your financial awareness. The more detailed you are about your income and expenses, the more realistic your budget becomes. It's more reflective of how you live and can help you identify areas where you can make changes. Next, I'll cover the following:

- Identifying all income sources.
- Tracking everything you spend.
- Calculating your available money.

Identify All Income Sources

Make a list of all your income sources. This is income after all taxes, deductions, and allocations are made prior to deposits in your checking account. This is money from your paycheck and from monthly interest and dividend income. Add all of these income sources together. Don't include income that is not regular monthly income (for example, bonuses, onetime payments, and income from freelance work).

Track Everything You Spend

Identify and track where your money goes. Include all monthly fixed expenses as well as occasional purchases. This includes the money you spend at the vending machine at your office, for example. Do this for a one-month period. This will give you the best real cost for your current lifestyle. You'll need this information to ensure you know where your money is going because some small expenses can add up to a substantial amount, which could be used to achieve your goals.

Do the following to determine your fixed and variable expenses:

- **Identify fixed expenses.** These include housing, utilities, transportation, cellphone service, subscription services, child care, gym memberships, student loans, credit card and debt payments, and insurance payments.
- **Identify variable expenses.** These include groceries, dining out, grooming, personal care, gasoline, tolls, entertainment, gifts, holiday spending, home and car maintenance, and other discretionary spending—as well as periodic fees and expenses, such as college tuition, insurance payments, and taxes.

After an entire month of tracking your expenses, be sure to categorize them. This will increase your awareness of how your expenses contribute to the different areas of your life. You can track your expenses by using any method that works for you. For example:

- Use a debit or credit card for all expenses.
- Process all payments through online bill pay.
- Get receipts for all purchases.

- Use your smartphone to keep track of any cash transactions.
- Use an app or budgeting software that tracks your expenses.

Calculate Your Available Money

To get the total cost of your living expenses, add your fixed and variable expenses together. The result is the total cost of your current spending habits.

Total Cost of Current Spending Habits = Fixed Expenses + Variable Expenses

Calculate your available money—also called cash flow—by taking your income and subtracting your expenses, as shown in the following equation. This calculation will help you to determine whether you're living within your means. Keep in mind that this number may not include contributions toward your financial goals.

Available Money = Income − Total Cost of Current Spending Habits

Next:

- **Analyze the results.** Do you have money available? If so, you're living within your means. This is cause for celebration, because any available money can be used toward your financial goals. If the opposite is true, then you're spending more than you make and may be relying on credit to pay for your monthly living expenses. With either result you'll want to make some choices that improve your situation.
- **Determine how you can increase your available money.** Can you reduce fixed expenses or eliminate some variable expenses? Ask yourself if particular expenses are ones you currently need or want. Are you willing to continue to pay for these services? Are they contributing to your vision for your life?

Rely on your growing awareness of what is truly important. The goal of this calculation is for you to determine how you can continue to pay for the things you value and remove the ones that don't matter. Now, make some choices:

- **When you have enough available money.** Use available money toward the financial goals you identified in step 3. You can use the available money to build your emergency fund, pay off debt, or invest in income-generating activities. Find additional ways to increase your available money.

■ **When you don't have enough available money.** It's time to make choices to improve your financial well-being. When you don't have enough available money, you have no funds to contribute to financial goals. However, you have two options: Increase income or decrease expenses. You can also do both—I certainly won't stop you.

Ask yourself these questions to help you determine different ways to increase your available money:

■ How can I increase my income?

■ Where can I cut expenses?

■ Can I cancel memberships and subscription services?

■ Am I able to refinance credit card debt, student loans, or both to lower payments?

Also, take a look at your net worth. Do you have cash or assets that can easily be converted to cash? Use the cash to pay off debt and eliminate monthly payments to increase your available money. Don't convert retirement funds and income-generating assets into cash to pay for monthly living expenses. Doing so will impact your long-term financial well-being.

You must prioritize what you spend money on and only pay for what's important. You'll find as you change your money mindset and make different lifestyle choices that cutting expenses may be easier for you to do, helping to increase your available money.

Step 5: Allocate Your Money

After reducing your expenses to reflect your values and the actual lifestyle you want to live, you'll see improvements in the amount of money you have available. This is an indication that you're on the road to financial wellness. It's now time to allocate your funds. Remember, money is earned to be spent—but how it's spent is the focus of this step.

Under the YOLO budget, your spending priorities are as follows:

- Pay yourself first.
- Pay living expenses.
- Eliminate debt.
- Spend money.
- Invest in income-generating assets.

Paying yourself first means prioritizing savings goals that improve long-term financial well-being. Paying yourself first is beneficial for motivation and reinforces good savings habits. After your savings goal contributions pay your living expenses, and then use additional money toward eliminating debt. When your current finances have improved and you're securing your future, you'll find it much easier to spend money without guilt and with more enjoyment. Use this calculation to determine the amount of spending money you can use as you choose:

Spending Money = Income − (Fixed Expenses + Financial Goals)

After you've contributed toward your goals and have fixed expenses covered, any additional money can be spent on more things that contribute to your lifestyle. The money can be used for pretty much anything you want, such as dinner with friends, a weekend getaway, spa services, or a concert. You can refer to this spending money as funds used for discretionary spending.

You only live once, and that means taking advantage of the right opportunities as they come along. That does not mean you should mindlessly and impulsively spend. Spending your paycheck should always have a purpose for your well-being. It should contribute to your enjoyment of your life. It should be used to grow your assets, increase your wealth, and manage your time. Again, with awareness of your spending habits and your values, you'll be prepared when the right opportunities to use money on the things and experiences that matter come along.

What's the most convenient way for you to spend your money?

Is it using cash or a debit card? Are you collecting rewards points? The mechanism you use to spend your money is less important than what you're spending it on. But I do get asked continually about what method of making purchases is preferred; that is, whether it's better to use cash or a debit card, or collect rewards points with a credit card.

I've found the answer to be simple: Use the method of payment that works for you. For some, switching from debit cards to cash has been helpful, while others continue to manage their finances quite well with credit cards. It does not matter what method you use to spend your money. If you haven't addressed your underlying money beliefs, your problem isn't your method of payment but your unchecked spending behavior.

Remain mindful of where your money is going and consider using a method of payment different from the one you currently use if it will support your budgeting efforts. Payment methods include cash; banking services such as checking accounts, debit cards, and online bill pay; and credit cards. Learn more about how each of the following payment methods can improve your situation:

- **Cash.** Use cash for your spending money—the money left after you've paid yourself and paid your monthly fixed and variable expenses. The cash in your wallet is a visual reminder of what you can spend in any given week or month. You may find yourself reluctant to spend the cash, in order to keep your wallet full. Rest assured that you need also feel no guilt if you decide to spend the cash on whatever you want at a given moment.

- **Bank or credit union.** Use online transfers, bill payments, and a debit card to make payments on your expenses. This will help you track details about where your money is being spent and will be useful in adjusting your budget if necessary. Using these services provides data that shows how you're spending money, so it's helpful for financial awareness.

- **Credit card.** When used correctly, a credit card can offer additional benefits. Many credit cards offer rewards points, so you could earn points or miles for spending on items you've budgeted for. You can then redeem these points as a reward for sticking with your budget. Although with credit cards you cannot spend more than your limit allows, be mindful that if spending to your limit exceeds your ability to pay your balance in full each month, you're creating debt.

Step 6: Monitor and Adjust Accordingly

The spending plan you create with the YOLO budget framework is reflective of your financial situation and lifestyle goals. To increase your spending on fun, determine where you can decrease fixed expenses, eliminate variable expenses, and increase income. This is a continual process and will improve over time.

As you track and monitor your budget, you may find the need to make some additional changes. This is to be expected. Your budget should evolve as goals are reached and changes to your lifestyle choices are made. The right budget allocates your money to maximize your enjoyment, not restrict it.

Review your budget on a monthly basis to determine if there have been changes to your financial situation. You can easily monitor your budget using an expense tracking app or website. Many financial institutions also offer personal financial management tools that can categorize your expenses and automate the tracking of your spending and saving. Use other budgeting tools that are easy for you to use. The key to budgeting success is engagement, which leads to more control over your money. Creating a budget can be life changing, but staying motivated can be challenging. Use these tips to stay motivated:

- Visualize success.
- Remain mindful of how you'll feel when goals are reached.
- Stay organized by tracking your progress.
- Be realistic and expect setbacks.
- Reward yourself along the way.

Since you've completed your budget framework, you should now have your lifestyle budget and spending plan. However, all great plans are worthless without a strategy to achieve them. In the next chapter we'll go over the purposeful money strategy, which will help you spend and save using a method using two checking accounts and an automated savings process.

CHAPTER 7

Using the Purposeful Money Strategy to Spend and Save

I n my first budgeting attempt, I set the right financial goals and was motivated to reach them. I changed my money mindset and began saving money. I cut expenses and was contributing 12 percent of my salary to my company's 401(k) plan. However, I found myself not achieving most of my goals and I still didn't feel in control of my money. I believed my budget was ineffective. I felt like a failure, so I abandoned the spending plan.

Over the years I've learned that I was not alone. My family and friends, along with countless people I've met, understood the importance of having a budget, and some of them had taken the time to create a budget, but they had either failed to implement the plan or to stick with it long term.

At an event in Lowell, Massachusetts, I had a conversation with Leo, a mechanic and single father. Leo had taken an important step by managing his finances with a budget, but he was still unsure of how to execute his plan.

"I have a budget, but what do I do next?" asked Leo.

"It's time to use it," I responded.

"How do I do that?" he said.

A lot of time is spent explaining the importance of budgeting and going through the steps to create a budget, but the lesson falls short in teaching people how to execute their budgets and integrate them into their daily lives.

Leo, like many others, is left to figure out how to make a budget work. A budget is only valuable if it's executed and can only work if it's implemented.

In my first attempt at budgeting, my spending plan was great, but I didn't have the right execution strategy to make it work long term. I needed a better way to manage money. I needed to visualize my progress and have control.

When I created the YOLO budget, I developed a strategy to automatically execute the spending plan and provide flexibility in how money is used. I believe that each dollar serves a purpose, and that if you use it for its intended purpose you'll be able to progress much more quickly toward your vision for your life.

After using the YOLO budget framework you learned about in Chapter 6, you should have a realistic budget that accounts for your real income, expenses, goals, and spending. To help with plan execution, use the purposeful money strategy to apply your budget to your spending and banking habits. In this chapter you'll learn about the dual checking accounts method and the purposeful savings method, which together will keep you mindful of your priorities, enable you to enjoy the present moment, and help you to achieve your future goals.

DUAL CHECKING ACCOUNTS METHOD

The dual checking accounts method separates your fixed expenses from your variable expenses. Fixed expenses are things such as mortgage or rent, car loan payments, utilities, and health-care and other insurance premiums. Fixed expenses are typically the same amount month to month. On the other hand, variable expenses are those that vary from month to month: For example, one month you may spend more on grooming and another month more on entertainment. There is also more spending flexibility within the variable expense category.

A few years ago I started using two different checking accounts for my expenses. I called one checking account my expense account and designated it for my fixed monthly expenses; the second I called my spending account and designated it for my variable expenses. My rent and car payments, for example, came out of the expense account. My spending money came out of the spending account.

It was easy to separate my expenses and using this method reduced my stress. I no longer worried that an unplanned ATM surcharge of $3.00 would cause an overdraft fee because a scheduled automatic payment had been processed. Using this dual checking account method, I gained control over my spending and banking habits because I had accounts set up for specific purposes.

As an unexpected positive result of having two checking accounts, I found myself more actively engaged in lowering my expenses. It became a competition of sorts to see how much more I could save by making changes to my fixed and variable expenses. I had an incentive to lower them. The additional money in my fixed account contributed toward reaching goals sooner, and the additional money in my variable account increased my available spending money.

After calculating your cash flow and getting specific details about your expenses, you will have two expense amounts—fixed and variable. To use the dual checking accounts method you will need to have two separate checking accounts, preferably at the same financial institution. Use the following steps to set up your dual checking accounts:

1. Open two checking accounts. One account will be used for fixed expenses and the other account for variable expenses.
2. Name these checking accounts accordingly (e.g., fixed and variable, or fixed expenses account and spending account).
3. Have your entire paycheck deposited into the checking account designated as your spending account via direct deposit.
4. Transfer the amount needed to cover your fixed expenses for the month into the checking account designated for fixed expenses.

You're most likely getting paid weekly or biweekly; therefore you'll need to transfer the correct amount per paycheck to cover your monthly fixed expenses. The remaining money in the checking account designated for variable expenses are funds you can spend more freely.

This dual checking account method will save you time and money by keeping your expenses separated and organized. Knowing that your fixed expenses are covered will give you peace of mind, and the money in your variable checking account can be spent as you wish with no guilt.

Expense Account

The expense account is the checking account where you keep money to pay all your fixed expenses. These expenses include all recurring monthly bills and contributions to your financial goals. This account should be used for expenses that are a bit more challenging to reduce and that you are contractually obligated to pay. For example, you'll pay your mortgage or rent, utilities, and car loan payments from this account. The money you contribute toward your savings, such as money for your emergency fund, will also come from the expense account.

Make it easier on yourself and set up automatic payments to creditors and service providers, and automatic transfers into your savings accounts. A debit card will not be needed for your expense account, but it can be useful if your creditors accept a debit card as a payment method. However, keep the debit card at home.

As you pay down your debt or work to reduce your fixed expenses, you should still have the same amount deposited each payday. You will then be able to use the extra money in the expense account toward your financial goals.

Spending Account

The spending account is used for all variable expenses. You should have a debit card for this checking account to make purchases. These purchases could include groceries, haircuts, personal-care products, gasoline, and tolls. How you spend the money in this account can vary from week to week and month to month. For example, one week you may spend more on groceries and the following week less because you had dinner at a restaurant with friends instead of cooking at home. Or one week you may be sick and stay home from work, which would mean less spent on gasoline and tolls but more on medicine.

This is also the account you'll tap into when you want to take that weekend getaway or go to the movies. However, it doesn't mean that you should just spend the money you have in this account mindlessly. It is not an accomplishment to see your spending-account balance at zero. Remember, every dollar you have should serve a purpose.

Similar to how you approach your expense account, as you continue to grow in awareness of how you're spending the money in your spending account, you'll be driven to cut your variable expenses down. This will result in more available money when the right opportunities come along—and they will come along. You can then confidently make purchases guilt free, without impacting your financial goals. If you find your spending account balance is growing because you're spending more mindfully, transfer some of that money into your expense account so it can go toward your goals.

 Action

Open two checking accounts at the same financial institution. Designate one account for your fixed expenses and one for your variable expenses, and set up your direct deposits accordingly.

THE PURPOSEFUL SAVINGS METHOD

Every dollar you save should be saved for a purpose. If you're saving money without a purpose in mind, you'll find yourself less motivated to reach your savings goals.

With my first budget, I decided my financial goals were to save for a home, a car, and retirement. At that time I didn't have a lot of money saved and I didn't have a proper method for saving money. I decided back then I would just save as much as I could in one savings account. I said to myself that the money saved in that account would be used for either a down payment on a house or a new car. I was proud of the amount of money that grew in that savings account.

Back then, I was advised to open a separate savings account with a different financial institution. The reasoning was that it would curb the temptation of using the savings for any purpose other than what it was intended for. The inconvenience of having a separate savings account outside of my primary financial institution meant I had limited access to the cash, keeping it safe from my mindless spending ways.

It was out of sight and out of mind.

I didn't have an ATM card attached to this savings account, and transferring money from that online savings account to my regular checking account took additional steps, and days to finalize. It was a purposeful inconvenience meant to keep me from withdrawing my savings.

Before I could buy a home or a new car, I began thinking of different ways to spend the money I was saving. When I wanted to buy something, the minor inconvenience did not keep me from using money in that savings account. I thought I was still doing okay because I'd continued to save money in that account. Unfortunately, when my financial situation changed I also found myself using the money in that savings account to pay for my living expenses.

Later on I realized that I had the right idea in saving money, but that I had executed my savings plan incorrectly. In the future I was going to have to define exactly what the money was going toward— and the more specific, the better.

Having a separate savings account that I allegedly couldn't touch was only a temporary fix. I used that solution to address an undiagnosed money mindset problem. There is merit in having a savings account that is more difficult to access, but when you're forcing yourself to save you're fighting against yourself, and you'll end up losing.

If you're saving money in an account that you've told yourself you cannot touch, answer this question:

Is this an attempt to force yourself to save?

Forcing yourself to save is definitely not the same as having a strong desire to save. You're not addressing the mindset that enables your financial behavior of using your savings at any given moment and for any reason.

As you've read this book, you've reshaped your money mindset and now understand the importance of awareness. You're now aware of how you're saving, what you're saving for, and the reason you're saving. Knowing what you're saving for is important, but knowing why you're saving is key to savings success. If it's for security, then an emergency fund is a priority. If it's for a home, then saving for a down payment is a must. If it's for relaxation, then a vacation club account is in order.

Be mindful that you're saving money for specific purposes—things that add value to your life. This purposeful approach to saving for the things that matter can help you achieve financial goals far sooner.

As I improved my money mindset and changed my financial behaviors, I took this awareness and opened separate savings accounts with my credit union.

I started with club savings accounts for vacation and holiday spending. With a club savings account I could contribute to the account at any time, but I was unable to touch the money until a specific date in the future. Because I knew I was saving for an all-inclusive resort vacation and Christmas presents for my family, I was encouraged to save $1,000 in each account. This purposeful approach to saving led to additional accounts with the same credit union.

I identified my goals: annual vacation, home ownership, luxury car, holiday presents, emergency fund, and savings accounts for my nieces and nephews. There were no account fees or minimum balance requirements, so the decision to have multiple savings accounts was easy.

My paycheck was deposited directly into the checking account designated for variable expenses. I also set up automatic transfers so that each payday money would be deposited into my fixed expenses checking account, to cover fixed monthly expenses, and into the following savings accounts:

- Emergency fund: $100
- Vacation club: $25
- Christmas club: $40
- Dream home club: $200
- My sexy car club: $100
- Nieces and nephews: $10

The rest of my paycheck that remained in the checking account designated for variable expenses I used for purchases.

The separate savings accounts offered the perfect visualization method to keep motivated with my savings goals. I could watch the accounts grow, and I knew exactly how I was going to use them. When I had additional money available, I would add it to one of the savings accounts. I found myself adding more into the vacation club, which aligned with my desire to have a lifestyle with lots of travel.

Since the money was immediately and automatically transferred each payday, I had little temptation to spend more than I could afford. For example, I wouldn't dare take money from my vacation club to buy a new pair of shoes. I valued travel more than a new pair of shoes.

I developed the purposeful savings method, which is based on my experiences with budgeting, to help others achieve their savings goals through a specific strategy. This savings strategy relies on your increased awareness of your values and financial goals. My money philosophy regarding savings is this: I'm saving money to spend money in the future.

When you accept this philosophy, you'll understand that how you spend money today can impact your ability to spend on something much more enjoyable in the future.

Think of everything you're saving for as something you've already purchased. It's similar to a layaway program, in which your item is placed on hold and only available to you once you've paid the full amount. This is a delayed gratification technique that uses the anticipation of a favored outcome to increase your enjoyment. When you anticipate getting something you really want, the waiting game can be much more exciting than the actual ownership. Think about the anticipation leading up to your birthday when you were a child. You knew you were getting gifts, but you also knew you'd have to wait until your birthday. That waiting period was exciting. When you opened your presents you were joyful, but weeks later the excitement might wane.

You are saving for a purpose, and you get to define that purpose. When you use the purposeful savings method, you're mindful of what, why, and how you'll save. For example, you might decide to set up an emergency fund based on the following goals:

- **What.** To save six months of living expenses to cover a period of unemployment or underemployment.
- **How.** By automatically depositing $50 to an emergency fund each payday.
- **Why.** To buy peace of mind and security in case of a period of unemployment or lost wages.

In this example, you've identified your purpose for saving. You understand that the money you save in an emergency fund is providing you peace of mind and security. This awareness will keep you from mindlessly using the fund, because you understand its actual value in your life. It's important to remember the reasons you save in order to stay on track and remain motivated.

Preparing for Purposeful Saving

Once you have a better understanding of why you are saving money, it becomes easier to decide what and how much to save. What and how you save depends on your financial goals and lifestyle choices. Use the following why, who, what, when, how, and where process to help you identify savings goals:

- **Why.** Be mindful of the emotional reasons you're making purchases today and your desire to make specific purchases in the future. Awareness of your why—your reason for saving—will help you prioritize savings goals. Are you making a purchase as a response to a bad workday? Are you spending due to financial habits such as bargain hunting?
- **Who.** Remember that the purchase is for someone—you or your child, your partner, family, or friend. The emotional bond that is connected with the purchase can influence your decision making and help you to place purposeful spending above mindless spending.
- **What.** Determine the price of your future purchases and link that to your specific savings goals. Everything has a price, whether it's a new smartphone or retirement. Analyze how much cash you need for each item. What is essential today? What purchases can be delayed?

- **When.** Commit to a deadline that is specific and measurable. The more specific you are, the more effectively you can increase the likelihood that you'll achieve your goal. You need to determine the savings time frame. Make necessary changes if you're off track.

- **How.** Decide how you'll save for each purpose. Will this be through payroll deduction? Will you utilize split deposits or automatic transfers? You'll learn which method works best and adjust accordingly.

- **Where.** Choose where you'll have these savings accounts. Find the right financial institution, one that offers multiple accounts, online transfers, and few or no fees. Then choose the type of account(s) to use, whether they are checking accounts, savings accounts, club accounts, money markets, CDs, or a combination of accounts.

Implementing Your Purposeful Savings Strategy

There are four steps in the purposeful savings strategy:

1. **Identify your savings goals.** Figure out which purchases you want to make and how soon you want to be able to make them. By following the process for preparing to save purposefully outlined above, you may have already gained clarity about the types of purchases you'll want to make. For example, you may want a newer car to have a reliable means of transportation and you've determined that you'd like to make this purchase within one to two years.

2. **Create a separate savings account for each purchase goal.** Name each savings account appropriately to remind yourself of its purpose. If you only have one savings account, it's harder to purposefully use the money for things you want. Be specific about the purchases you want to make.

   For example, instead of using the generic label *savings account* or *emergency fund*, the name of your savings account could be as specific as *six months of security*. Or you could be more detailed and include your target amount; for example, *six-month emergency fund with $6,000 goal.* Having specific names can help reinforce your awareness of the purpose for each account when you review them.

3. **Automate the savings transfer each pay period.** Have your paycheck deposited directly into your checking account and set up automatic transfers for each payday. This will simplify the savings process and keep you on track. When you set up automatic transfers, the system will move money from your checking account into your various savings accounts based on the amount you've allocated.

    For example, if your net paycheck is $1,000 each payday, you might set it up so that after each direct deposit the system will transfer $50 into your emergency fund, $25 into your vacation club, and so on.

4. **Monitor your progress and adjust.** Your situation and financial goals can change. It's important to remain mindful of those changes and how they'll impact your vision for your life. Make the necessary adjustments that align with your changing situation. If you want something sooner, it may mean allocating more money toward your savings goal and reducing a transfer for another goal.

    For example, if you were able to reduce your living expenses by $100 per month, you'd have an additional $100 to spend as you wish or contribute to future purchases. You could also choose to spread the $100 evenly among all savings goals.

I've found this to be an effective strategy for all savings goals: You're spending money on things that add value in your life, and you can see the progress along the way. This will keep you motivated and inspired to stick with your budget and reach your savings goals. Be realistic about your savings goals. For example, you can't expect to save $10,000 for a mortgage down payment in 24 months if you haven't been able to save $1,000 in one year. It's certainly possible to save $10,000 as a down payment, but it takes continued purposeful intent to achieve. Don't set yourself up for failure. As your financial situation changes and habits improve, adjust your savings goals accordingly.

Purposeful Savings Strategy Categories

There are six types of savings categories that I use in the purposeful savings strategy. You don't need to use all of them, but they can help you identify and prioritize what's important to you.

Emergency Fund

A very important part of the purposeful savings strategy is protecting your financial well-being during periods of unemployment and uncertainty. This is done with an emergency fund. It's recommended that you have six months of living expenses in a savings account that's easily accessible or in assets that you can easily convert to cash.

You don't need to save six months of your income. Instead, you need to have six months of living expenses in an emergency fund. This means that the lower your living expenses are, the smaller the amount in this fund will be. That's another incentive to keep your lifestyle choices in line with your financial goals.

Although the main purpose of an emergency fund is to provide financial stability during periods of lost wages, you can use money to pay for other unplanned events, such as the need to replace the engine in your car. However, you need to replace whatever you take out of your emergency fund as soon as possible. To grow your emergency fund, remind yourself that every deposit is buying you peace of mind in the face of an uncertain future. My money philosophy includes this truism: Emergencies do happen. It's not a matter of if, but a matter of when.

Immediate Savings

The time frame associated with immediate savings goals is usually under 12 months and it changes annually. Immediate savings are goals for taxes, annual vacations, holiday spending, gift giving, and sales events. Think of these items as things that happen annually and set savings goals to plan for them. The number of savings accounts and the amount you'll need to save will vary. What expenses do you have to pay each year? What things do you want to purchase within a year?

Short-Term Savings

Short-term savings are for goals with time frames of between one and two years. These are based on wants and needs that you've identified and purchases you plan to make in the near future. This category might include savings for new equipment for a hobby or a side business. Or it may include savings that allow you to move to a new city or buy new furniture. If there are things that add value in your life, you definitely should buy them by saving for them.

Mid-Term Savings

Mid-term savings goals usually have a time frame of between two and five years. This category tends to be for larger ticket items or so-called dream goals, such as buying a new car, planning for a big wedding, or taking a once-in-a-lifetime trip. When you're thinking about your purposes for your money, be mindful of the things and experiences you want to have and determine when you'd like for them to happen. For example, let's say you want a new car and are financially able to spend $250 per month on financing. If your current car is still in working condition, instead of buying the car today you might decide to keep your car for three more years and deposit that $250 into your future-car savings account. In three years you would have saved $9,000 toward the goal of a new car.

Long-Term Savings

Long-term savings goals relate to your vision for your life. I view long-term savings as the opportunity to save money to achieve life-changing goals and put the time frame for achieving them at between 5 and 10 years, but your time frame could be shorter or longer. These goals include saving for a home, starting a family, beginning a new career, starting a business, and saving for a child's college education. By setting long-term savings goals, you've quantified parts of your dream lifestyle. This makes it easier to make progress.

Retirement Savings

Retirement savings include savings, insurance, investments, and income-generating assets that will cover the cost of your living expenses during a period in which you no longer exchange time for a paycheck. The earlier you start saving for retirement, the more money you'll have at the typical retirement age. With regard to your retirement savings, contribute to your company's 401(k) plan and start a Roth IRA. There are other strategies you can employ, which will be covered later in this book. My money philosophy about retirement is this: We're all going to need to retire someday, and some of us get to retire sooner than others.

What do you want to save for? Think about the things and experiences you want to have in this lifetime.

 Action

Identify one savings goal for each of the purposeful savings categories. Start with the amount you'll need for an emergency fund.

As you read about the purposeful money strategy, you might have been thinking about another financial goal—getting out of debt. I understand that it can be a challenge to think of saving money when you have debt. However, it is important to pay yourself first and prioritize saving to keep you motivated and on track for living your dream lifestyle. In the next chapter we'll go over how to eliminate the debt ball and chain forever, by changing your relationship with credit and by using a motivational approach to debt repayment.

8

Improving Credit Use and Eliminating Debt Forever

The most effective debt-elimination strategy is a change of mindset. A few years ago, I was managing my finances based on my credit score. I was young and uninformed. I had a score in the high 700s and held a stable job. I would apply for credit and get approved. I judged my financial well-being by my ability to get approved for credit. At the time, I really thought that this was what it meant to manage finances well. However, my reliance on credit to supplement my lifestyle soon resulted in debt.

I remember looking at my credit card statements and wondering why the balances remained the same. So I did what I thought was a smart financial move: I consolidated my debt into one loan. My six credit card statements were consolidated into one payment per month. I rejoiced at the idea that I would be debt free in 36 months. But that's not the way things worked out. Instead, I eventually found myself with a debt-consolidation loan payment and new credit card payments.

I thought I had resolved my original credit card problem, but consolidating my debt hadn't addressed the underlying issue that caused the debt in the first place: my money mindset. Without addressing your mindset on credit and debt, no debt elimination strategy will remain effective. The debt cycle will continue.

Eliminating debt doesn't just improve your financial life, it improves your entire life. If you're holding debt, then you may find it more difficult to leave a job you dislike. If you're still making payments on purchases you no longer value, then you may be unable to afford the things that matter. The feeling of being shackled by the debt ball and chain can make anyone see the future as hopeless.

On the road to financial wellness, debt is the huge roadblock that's keeping you from progressing toward your destination. At times, no matter how you look at this roadblock, it may seem absolutely impossible to get around it. You feel stuck and exhausted. During my road-trip workshops, many people shared with me that debt was ruining their lives. Their sleep was becoming more and more restless. Every attempt they made to get out of debt had resulted in failure. At one workshop I had a private conversation with a woman in her 30s named Jessica.

"I wouldn't be in debt if I made more money," said Jessica.

"Why do you think income is the problem?" I asked.

"Well, if I made more, I could pay off the balances," she responded.

"What made you spend more than you make?" I inquired.

Jessica looked at me with confusion. I could see she wanted to share a thought but was unable to speak. A man who was listening in on our conversation joined in.

"I'm in debt up to my eyeballs," the man stated. "I don't know why they kept increasing my limit."

"You weren't forced to use the new available credit," I said.

"I had emergencies that came up and so I used it," he replied.

Jessica placed responsibility for her debt on her income, while this man placed it on creditors. Without addressing their money mindsets, it was impossible to eliminate their debt, because their beliefs continued to enable them to make excuses to use credit. In Jessica's case, her mindless spending was the problem, not her income. As for the man who interrupted our conversation, the issue wasn't his creditors, but his lack of available savings.

Your mindset plays an important role in a debt-elimination strategy. Before you start thinking about balance transfers, consolidation loans, or the debt snowball method or debt avalanche method, you need to further understand your scarcity mindset. Get clear about your relationship with credit and debt by answering the following questions:

- What beliefs do you hold about debt?
- Why haven't you been able to eliminate debt?
- Why are you reliant on credit?

In Jessica's situation, she held on to the belief that a higher salary would remedy her debt problems. She believed all attempts to get out of debt would not work unless she made more money. Jessica already felt defeated and this gave her the excuse to do nothing until she made more money, thus placing the responsibility for eliminating debt on someone else—for instance, her manager, who controlled her pay raises.

It may give us temporary comfort to believe we're victims of circumstance. Instead of reminding yourself why you cannot do something, start thinking of how you can make it happen. When you believe that it's impossible to get out of debt unless certain conditions are met then you won't find the right method to eliminate debt.

An unhealthy money mindset will keep you in debt. It perpetuates a belief that your debt is the result of someone else's decision. For example, the creditor's decision to increase the man's credit limit was based on guidelines that the lender set. If the man had followed a money philosophy, he would have used it to decide whether or not to use the new credit limit.

I follow this money philosophy regarding credit: Just because I've been approved for credit does not mean I can afford to use the credit.

Debt *is* a result of your decisions, and the power to get out of debt rests in your hands as well. As you're building your YOLO budget, debt elimination should be a priority. To repeat myself: Debt reserves your future time for work rather than fun. Reinforce good savings habits by paying yourself first. Then tackle debt with your changed money mindset. Accept that you've made unwise decisions with credit. This acceptance will keep you aware and mindful of your priorities.

Here are some ways to change your mindset regarding credit and begin following the right debt-elimination strategy:

- **Identify the root cause.** Acknowledge your past mistakes and take responsibility for the fact that your debt is the result of how you used credit. Practice self-awareness to understand the root causes of your credit use. Why are you spending money you don't have? Why couldn't you delay the purchase for another time? Why was it important to buy the item? If you believe that another person caused the debt, ask yourself why you allowed it to happen.

- **Review your cash-flow number.** Your income did not cause you to go into debt. Your spending and reliance on credit contributed to your debt. If your expenses are higher than your income, then you may be relying on credit to fill the gap. The continued use of credit to pay for living expenses will keep you in debt. Be mindful of your vision for your life, and begin to cut expenses that don't contribute to the lifestyle you want to live.

- **Stay focused on your vision.** You must have a clear vision for your life and an awareness of the lifestyle you want to live. This will help you overcome the motivational challenges of paying off debt from old purchases that no longer matter. Remember, you're not paying for something old, but rather buying something new: a better future. Remain mindful that every dollar used to pay off debt is lessening the weight of that debt ball and chain.

- **Follow your money philosophy.** Make the right decisions that create the lifestyle you want to live. Have clarity about your values so that you can easily decide what are needs and what are wants. Stay committed and positive. Believe the light that you're seeing in your dark space is the light at the end of the tunnel, not the light of a train barreling toward you.

- **Remember you have control.** Debt can make you feel powerless, but you have more leverage than you think. You have to be proactive, not reactive. Reach out to your creditors and negotiate for better interest rates or a better repayment plan. Tackle one debt at a time, and communicate with all parties involved. You have options, including debt consolidation, repayment plans, settlement agreements, and even bankruptcy.

As you take on debt with a healthier money mindset, you need to determine which tools and strategies can help you to achieve your goal. If you're considering balance transfers, consolidation loans, and refinancing options, remember that these are not solutions—they're tools to help with your efforts. Be mindful that moving debt from one type of loan to another is just shuffling the balance around, not eliminating it. However, awareness about balance transfers, refinancing, and debt consolidation can be helpful in your debt-elimination efforts. These tools can lower monthly payments and the total interest you'll pay, resulting in savings that can be used toward debt repayment.

There are many different types of debt. The most common are student loans, credit cards, personal loans, auto loans, and mortgages. Not all debt is created equal. Some debts should be paid first. For example, credit card debts should be eliminated first. This type of debt is created from buying things on credit. You might even still be paying for something that you no longer use. Credit card debt serves no purpose aside from being a constant reminder of your mindless spending ways.

After you eliminate your credit card debt, pay off personal loans that are not attached to assets. Then set your sights on paying off your student loans. There may be tax benefits to the interest you're paying, but don't hold on to loans because of those benefits. Consider student-loan consolidation or refinancing to lower rates and simplify repayment. Finally, pay off loans associated with your car and home. These loans are tied to an asset. Prioritize paying off your car loan first, as it is a depreciating asset. Once you've paid the car loan, you may be able to lower your insurance premiums too.

CREDIT CARD DEBT

Credit cards enable you to buy the things that you want now; however, they can impact your future ability to buy the things that matter later. A credit card balance is the type of debt ball and chain that continues to grow whether or not you're making additional purchases. Credit use creates a fake reality. It makes us believe we own something, but it's really the other way around. We're owned by the purchases we've made. We become indebted to the things we've bought, requiring us to make payments for years, very often for a period surpassing the usable life of the product.

I wanted to address credit card debt in more detail because a credit card is a financial tool that's often misused. At one point in my life I had 13 credit cards. Because of my sound but unwise credit use, creditors offered me the unlimited potential to spend. I had three American Express cards, a Discover card, multiple bank and credit-union credit cards, department store and gas cards, and a number of credit cards used for accruing airline points. And I had a balance due on each of them.

Credit card debt is the cause of so much stress and unhappiness. You make the minimum monthly payment, but only see the balance decrease by a few dollars. And if a payment is made just a few days past the due date, you see all the gains from your previous monthly payments vanish.

I have a money philosophy about credit cards: The credit card promise relies on the availability of credit, but once used, it no longer serves a purpose.

When your financial goal is to pay off credit card debt, the most reasonable step is not adding to it. Keep the credit cards out of your wallet. Use every extra dollar you have to pay the balances down. Negotiate with your creditors for better interest rates, and consider your options for consolidating or transferring balances. To avoid late payment fees, make your minimum monthly payments on time, every time. And I highly recommend that you pay the monthly amount that allows you to pay off the debt in three years. It is required by federal law that credit card issuers list this amount, which can be found on your credit card statement.

Did you receive a bonus from work?

You might be tempted to start investing in the stock market or adding to your savings if you get a bonus, but if you're paying over 20 percent on your credit card balance and only making 0.5 percent interest on a savings account, you may want to consider using that unexpected income toward debt repayment. All things considered, you're already paying yourself first with your paycheck, so any additional money should be used on another YOLO budget priority: debt elimination.

What if you have debt spread across multiple credit cards?

There are two methods of paying off credit card debt. The first recommends that you pay off the balance with the highest interest rate first—a prudent financial move—while the second argues that you should pay off the smallest balance first. These methods are called the debt avalanche method and the debt snowball method, respectively. I will discuss both of these methods in further detail, but know that both options require you to continue to make payments on all credit cards while you focus debt repayment toward one card at a time. Remember that debt elimination is a financial and mental process. The method that you choose to pay off credit card debt should be the method that motivates you to eliminate debt.

USING THE DEBT AVALANCHE METHOD

The debt avalanche method targets debt with the highest interest rate first, regardless of the size of the credit card balance. Once you've paid off the debt with the highest interest rate, you move on to the one with the next highest rate. You apply all prior payments from the paid-off debt to the next debt, essentially creating an avalanche.

Here's how this method works:

1. List all of your debts, starting with the balance with the highest interest rate and continuing in descending order.
2. Focus on repayment of the debt with the highest interest rate first, while making minimum payments on the other debts.
3. Apply the payments from the first debt (now paid off) to the next debt, and so on.

Table 8.1 shows an example of using the debt avalanche method to pay off three credit card balances.

Table 8.1 Sample Credit Card Debt Repayment Plan Using the Avalanche Method

	Balance	Interest Rate	Minimum Payment
Credit Card #1	$5,000	20.99%	$89
Credit Card #2	$500	14.99%	$20
Credit Card #3	$6,300	9.99%	$121

In this example, you would pay as much as you can on credit card #1, which in this case is $89 a month. Once that credit card is paid off, you would add that $89 to the $20 minimum payment for credit card #2. This becomes a payment of $119 (you can choose to add more to the payment as well). While paying off credit card #2, you'd continue to pay the $121 minimum monthly payment on credit card #3. After completely paying off credit card #2, you would then use the payments from credit cards #1 ($89), #2 ($20), and #3 ($121) to make the monthly payment on credit card #3 (a total of $240). After strict adherence to these monthly payments, you'll find that you've avalanched your way out of debt.

This method might make the most financial sense because you're prioritizing paying off debt with higher interest rates, and higher rates cost you more. However, as I've discussed previously, debt elimination has a lot more to do with your mindset than with the numbers themselves.

USING THE DEBT SNOWBALL METHOD

In contrast, the debt snowball method, you're choosing to pay off the smallest debt balances first. Once you've paid off the smallest debt, you then apply those payments to the next smallest, and so on. You'll eventually have more available money to pay toward the larger debts. Think of your increasing payments as a snowball that grows as it goes down a hill adding more snow.

Here's how this method works:

1. List all your debts, starting with the one with the smallest balance.
2. Focus on complete repayment of the debt with the smallest balance first, while making minimum payments on your other debts.
3. Apply the same payments you made on the first debt (now paid off) to the next debt, and so on.

Table 8.2 shows an example of using the debt snowball method to pay off three credit card balances.

Table 8.2 Sample Credit Card Debt Repayment Plan Using the Snowball Method

	Balance	Minimum Payment
Credit Card #1	$500	$25
Credit Card #2	$6,300	$146
Credit Card #3	$7,000	$200

In this example, you would pay $25 a month toward credit card #1, which is the minimum payment plus what you've determined is the maximum extra amount you can pay. Once that credit card is paid off, you would add that $25 payment into the minimum payment of $146 for credit card #2. Your monthly payment on credit card #2 would then become a payment of $171 (you can choose to add more to the payment as well). While paying off credit card #2, you'd continue to pay the minimum payment of $200 for credit card #3. After you've completely paid off credit card #2, you would then use the payments from #1 ($25), #2 ($146), and #3 ($200) to make the monthly payments on credit card #3 (a total of $371 per month).

This method does not make the most financial sense, because the larger balances may be accruing more interest, in which case you will end up paying more overall. However, this method is best for those who are motivated in this way. As the snowball increases in size, the excitement builds, and the momentum continues to grow.

The best method for you to use is the one that motivates you the most. Choose one method first, and if that doesn't seem to excite you about repaying your debt faster, choose another method.

When I was tens of thousands of dollars in debt from credit cards, I wanted to see at least one credit card with a zero balance, and the fastest way for that to happen was to pay off the smallest balance first. I paid off the $500 balance on my gas card. After seeing that balance at zero, I was motivated to pay off the $1,000 balance on a department store card, and I worked my way up to the credit cards with larger balances. This approach made me feel as if I had accomplished something, because I saw immediate results. It became an obsession to see how fast I could get the other balances to zero. At the time I believed that I had created the best strategy to get out of credit card debt—until I was told that this method already existed and it was called the debt snow-ball method, as I have just explained to you.

Debt is your ball and chain, and no matter what type of debt you have, your future time is allocated to that financial obligation. Remain mindful of how you're using credit and prioritize debt repayment over any future purchases. Once you experience freedom from debt you'll feel empowered, knowing that the money you're making can be invested into growing your assets and protecting your interests.

It's now time to take full control of your life, and I'll help you learn how to do so in the next part of this book. In the following chapters you'll apply what you've been learning to a daily routine of purpose-ful living.

PART **IV**

Taking Control

A mentor of mine once said that I should work to "live fully but die broke." In order to live fully, our finances have to be in order. It means ensuring that money can last to the final moments of life, and that requires control—in making enough money, spending on the right things, protecting what matters, and investing instead of mindlessly consuming.

This gives us the opportunity to control our time and do more of the things that matter. "Live fully but die broke" was my mentor's definition of "living once." It has since become one of my guiding money philosophies.

The major life-changing belief I gained on my personal road to financial wellness is that I had more control over my life. I could control how I spent my time and money. I could control the types of conversations I had. And I could choose my financial relationships, because I had control over deciding what was right for me. My growing awareness made it clear that today is as good as any other day to enjoy life, and that I could strike a balance between now and tomorrow—by taking control.

As you've been reading this book, you've increased your awareness and learned how to create a plan—it's now time for you to take control. Taking control happens through actions that get you from where you are today to where you want to be—living your dream lifestyle.

Your goal is not to just to make it through the day, but rather to live a rich and purposeful life. You can't spend your way to happiness, and you can't live fully when you're indebted to others. You don't want to live with too little, and you don't want to leave with too much.

When you're in control of your thoughts, time, and money, you'll find yourself doing more of the things you want to. You'll have control over how much you make, how much you spend, and how you live.

There are many things we can't control, but there are many more things that we can. We cannot control the weather, but we can control what we wear. We cannot control the behaviors of others, but we can control how we respond. We cannot control how banks operate, but we do control the decision of whether to use them. In other words, you can control what you think and how you respond to people, things, and situations.

I've often heard people use the phrase "It is what it is." This statement supports the belief that we have no control over our lives and our finances. We can't fix our financial situation or credit problems because it is what it is. We're unhappy with our jobs and feel trapped, but it is what it is. We've accepted that we have no control, so we don't get to exercise control.

Remember, this is your life, and you don't have to live with bad credit or stay with a job that makes you unhappy. You have a choice, and every day you're making decisions that are keeping you in the same situation. Increasing your awareness will open your mind to the opportunities that are around you to make different decisions and take control of your financial life.

You take control through actions.

In the last three chapters of this book, you'll learn how to live purposefully by taking specific actions to manage many aspects of your life. I'll go over how you can regain control over your time, how you can spend consciously, how to improve your financial relationships, and how to live mindfully.

CHAPTER **9**

Creating a
Purposeful Life

Our mindsets are shaped by the people closest to us, but in general they are cultivated by society's values. We're a society that places importance on consumption. As consumers, we are made to believe that we are in control. In order to exercise that control, we must consume. If we are not consuming, we're made to feel less like a member of society. We may feel rejected and ostracized. Yet each and every day we applaud and praise those who break societal norms and those who dare to live their dreams.

I've discovered that we have the power to create our own realities. But if we're too busy consuming to have time for creating, then we'll never reach our full potential. The money mindsets we hold and the financial decisions we make can perpetuate a lifestyle of consumption. It's a cycle that's difficult to break if you remain unaware of the opportunity to be a creator. Creating gives you a sense of accomplishment, a sense that you're contributing to the world around you and are shaping the reality in which you live.

We buy many things to convince ourselves that our hard work means something, but the things we consume can strap us to a life we don't want. So we work harder and spend more time doing things we have to do than things we want to do. Consuming goods is not a goal—it's just a fact of life. However, consuming more goods than you can enjoy is a waste of your time.

As a result of my backpacking trip around the world, I realized I could define my purpose. I became aware that life's meaning was not to be found in exploring different countries but rather was based on the purpose I chose. I learned I had control over that choice. My biggest lesson: I have control over creating a purposeful life. And you do too.

A *purposeful life* is one in which you're maximizing the time spent on opportunities for a dream life and a better society. You're mindful in the present moment and aware of the past and future. Once you define what *living once* means for you, it will change how you manage time, prioritize the things you do, and choose the conversations you have and the people you surround yourself with.

It will transform your life of mere existence into a *life of purpose*. As I've discussed throughout this book, you have control over creating the vision for your life and *can* define a purpose for it.

FINDING HAPPINESS

Despite all the twists and turns in my journey, overall I've lived in a state of happiness. There are days when I feel less happy and other days when I am filled with abundant joy. I've learned happiness isn't a product or a destination. Happiness is a feeling.

And, *happiness is a choice*. You can choose to be happy.

You can increase your happiness by knowing and accepting that you *have* control over deciding what contributes to your happiness. Your increase in awareness, and creating a plan, are both necessary steps for you to take control of living your vision for your life and creating more happiness in it.

During the road trip a man in his late twenties shared that he had believed buying a condo would make him happy. He had followed a conventional path in life and now found himself in a state of unhappiness.

"I was really excited when I was looking to buy a condo," he said, and then added, "I was happy when I closed on the home and moved in."

"What happened a year later?" I asked.

"Not much, really. I felt good about owning my condo, but after a year I felt tied down to my job," he responded.

"What were you feeling?" I inquired.

"I wasn't as happy as I had been before, and right now I feel I have no choice but to keep a job I haven't enjoyed for some time," he answered.

In this man's case, he was dissatisfied at work and believed he could purchase his happiness by buying a condo. He believed his happiness was tied to owning a condo, and that, unfortunately, didn't align with his values. He was unaware of the vision for his life and the lifestyle he wanted to live. This man does have options, though: He could sell his condo, find a more satisfying job, or rent his home. What I hope to illustrate is that you have choices and control over your situation at more moments in your life than you might otherwise think.

Happiness cannot be purchased and it isn't given. You cannot spend your way to happiness. And you cannot expect other people or things (partner, family, friends, job) to give you happiness. Happiness is based on what's happening internally, not externally. It comes from your thoughts and feelings—your mindset.

Have you ever received a gift from a loved one that made you happy? And conversely, have you received a gift from the same loved one that didn't? Understand that nothing about receiving a gift from the gift giver has changed—that person gave you something, whether from love or obligation. Your thoughts and feelings at that given moment might be different, though. Your happiness might have had nothing to do with the actual gift, but with how you perceived the gift to be meeting *your* needs and wants—which are ever changing—at a given time.

Happiness does matter in living a purposeful life. You can do the following to create more happiness:

- Change your mindset and choose to focus on the positive. Your awareness of change can help you control its impact on your life.

- Work toward your vision for your life. When you're making progress on your hopes and dreams, you'll find happiness along the way.

- Be mindful of what you want to do and do more of it. You can't do it all, but you certainly can do more of the things that matter to you.

- Remain true to your values. The more you stick to what you value, the happier you will become.

- Spend your time on things you love. Choose the people and projects that add value in your life.

- Choose to create more experiences instead of consuming more goods.

 Action

List five items on your bucket list that you want to accomplish in one to two years. After listing them, determine how they contribute to your happiness and make them a part of your spending plan.

INCREASING YOUR AWARENESS

I've talked at length about awareness throughout this book. Cultivating awareness is not a onetime exercise. It must be practiced daily. The more you know about your situation, the better informed you are to make the best decisions in creating the life you want to live.

It might be easier to have someone tell you what to do, but that hands the control over to someone else. You can take control through adding to your knowledge. Make an effort to increase your knowledge of who you are and what you enjoy.

Become informed, not just entertained.

Prioritize learning about finances and self-development. You'll make financial and life decisions that are better informed. The more information you expose yourself to, the better equipped you'll be to progress toward your vision for your life.

Take control of your mind and emotions. We're taught to take the emotion out of decisions involving money, but money is quite personal. No matter how many times you're told that you should simply look at the numbers, you might find yourself ignoring the numbers and making decisions based on emotion—intentionally or not.

Have you ever been in a situation in which you knew that product A was a better value for its price, but product B was emotionally appealing to you? Control isn't about suppressing your emotions; it's about being aware of what's causing those emotions and responding mindfully.

The more you know about money, the better decisions you will make. It lessens the amount of future stress. It might feel stressful to think about the amount of information you need to know: information about banking, accounting, investments, and real estate. It sounds overwhelming, but wealthy and purposeful people seek to know what's important and what resources are available.

Increasing your financial awareness and self-awareness is a continuous process, one in which you need to remain proactive. Being proactive will help you regain control over certain aspects of your life. The more you know about finances, the more clearly you will be able to focus on the right things, the things that allow you to live a rich and purposeful life. Increase your awareness by doing the following:

- Review your financial statements periodically and understand the terms of your accounts, as well as the fees you pay.
- Request your credit reports and review them annually.
- Read self-development books to improve your skills and challenge your thinking, in order to grow as an individual.
- Subscribe to financial blogs and podcasts, ask questions, and seek financial understanding (not just answers).
- Talk with friends and family about money in a mindful way, focusing on lessons, not judgments.
- Learn about financial programs offered by the government, nonprofits, and your employer and use appropriate services to your benefit.

▼ Action

Read one personal finance or self-development book a month.

ORGANIZING YOUR FINANCES

My life, like my finances, used to be in disarray. I was disorganized. I was out of control, and my environment reflected my inner reality. I once found a $150 refund check in an unopened letter among a pile of papers, magazines, and notepads. I had almost missed the date by which the check had to be deposited. I remember thinking to myself about how wasteful I was and that I needed to organize my life.

I used to think having paper documents and statements meant I was in control, because I could physically touch paper. In reality, though, all that did was create clutter. So, I established a new e-mail address and opted for online statements. I decluttered and shredded all the paper documents that were piled in my room. For my online accounts, I selected the option to receive text alerts or e-mail messages when statements, disclosures, and notices were available.

I set up e-mail rules to keep my personal in-box at zero, which meant e-mails from my family and friends would be prioritized. I cleaned my desktop and removed all downloaded files and documents that I hadn't opened within the last two years. I created a better folder system for all my photos. I used an online vault to store copies of important documents, such as my passport and Social Security card. (As a side note, having an electronic copy of my passport online proved helpful when I was traveling overseas.)

When I decided to take control of my finances I wanted to make it easy and simple, so I would be thinking less about when to make a payment and more about how to get out of debt. I called my bank, credit union, creditors, and other financial services organizations to figure out what options I had to simplify my finances.

I simplified my credit cards and signed up for electronic billing statements. I changed my credit card billing dates so that they were all the same day, or at least within the same week. I set up transaction alerts to be kept informed of charges, payments, and fraud through text messages. My payments were automatically transferred from my checking account.

In terms of banking, I made some additional changes to simplify my finances: I chose one financial institution to do the majority of my banking with. I had my paycheck deposited directly into my checking account and set up automatic transfers. I used online bill pay so that I would receive all of my electronic bills in one place, including bills for my cellphone, utilities, and student loan. I also opted for online account statements and text alerts to keep me informed. I kept a debit card and only one credit card in my wallet.

I downloaded a free credit report–monitoring app that kept me informed of changes in my credit report that needed my immediate attention. This kept me organized and up-to-date about my credit. I designated the first day of spring as the time for an annual review of my credit report.

I opted out of all third-party and prescreened offers and placed my cellphone number on the Do Not Call registry (go to DoNotCall.gov). This prevented unsolicited offers from being sent to me and lessened the temptation to get new credit cards or services I didn't need.

In automating as much of your finances as possible, you are taking control. You will no longer be scrambling to run to the bank to deposit your check or waiting on the phone to make transfers, and the fear of getting hit with a late-payment fee is reduced when payments are automatic.

When you've organized your finances, you'll spend less time on trivial tasks and have more time to spend on purposeful pursuits. Take advantage of all available tools to organize your finances. You can organize and simplify your life by doing the following:

- Choose a primary financial institution.
- Set up your direct deposits, automatic transfers, bill paying, and transaction alerts.
- Opt-in with all your service providers to receive statements electronically and have them sent to a specific e-mail folder.
- Unsubscribe from useless e-mails and set rules for your e-mail in-box.
- Use a personal financial management tool or an account aggregation service to view all your banking and credit accounts in one place.
- Download a free credit report monitoring app.

Action

Answer this question: How can you gain control by reorganizing your financial life?

MANAGING YOUR TIME

Time is an asset and must be managed if you are to live a purposeful life. I want you to understand that there are two types of time: clock time and real time. We all have the same amount of seconds, minutes, and hours in a given day. And we have 365 days in a year. The amount of hours I have in a day is no different from the amount of hours you have.

In contrast, real time is relative and based on your mindset. When you're having fun, time seems to fly by, and when you're doing something you don't enjoy, time seems to drag on.

I believe the reason that many of us have been unable to manage time is that we're trying to control clock time, which cannot be controlled. We cannot add more hours in the day. However, you can manage real time and accomplish many of the goals you've set. If you're clear about your values and your goals, you'll always find the time to make progress toward your vision. Managing real time removes the mindset that there is not enough time, or that it's not the right time, or that you've run out of time.

Do you want more control over your life?

Think about how you're managing your time. There are 168 hours in the week, and if 40 hours of your week are spent at work, then you have 128 hours to do as you please. You might have no control on the work you're required to do within the 40-hour workweek, but you have more control over how you manage real time. You can decide how much time you'll devote to your personal growth, relationships, and financial goals. Use your time to *invest* in yourself. You are the most important thing in your world. Strive to be the best thing you can be for yourself and your loved ones. That means investing time into expanding your knowledge, experiences, and network.

It is okay to spend some time watching shows, scrolling through social media, and playing video games, but if you're spending more time doing those activities than anything else, you're wasting your life. I want you to remove the limiting thoughts of clock time and focus on what you're doing in real time.

Do you want a new career or to achieve certain financial goals?

Invest your time into learning a new skill or perhaps a new language. Use your time to write, paint, or create music. Go out and network with interesting people who are doing the amazing things you'd like to do. When you're learning or doing something you enjoy, you're managing your time effectively.

Do you want peace of mind?

We're so busy filling our time with tasks and external stimulation that taking a moment to be still and present is refreshing. Give yourself a break, and meditate and self-reflect. Spend a few minutes in the middle of the day to clear your thoughts. Sit back in your chair and close your eyes. Take deep breaths and concentrate on your breathing. Just five minutes of quiet and calm can give you a fresh outlook.

The benefit of self-reflection has been evident in my life. It has helped me to increase my awareness and gain peace of mind. I no longer get consumed by my thoughts or feel anxiety or high levels of stress. Through self-reflection, I am able to reassess the day or a situation. This helps me to learn more about why I acted in a certain way, or how I reacted to people or news. Manage your time by knowing how much of it was spent thinking about situations and conversations, serving no purpose other than keeping you from working on things that matter.

Do you want to have more time to do what matters?

One way to get back some of your time is to pay someone else to take care of one or more chores (if that's within your budget, of course).

A few years ago I hired someone to do my laundry. With four loads and one washing machine and one dryer, it was taking me four hours to complete this task. It cost $60 to have someone else wash, dry, and fold my laundry. At the time I was making around $40 per hour. Doing the laundry myself, I would have spent $160. Since I paid someone else to do the task, it only cost $60. If you have tasks that need to be completed, find someone else to do them for you. Tasks and chores that are necessary but don't add value should be delegated. You could be investing that time into taking a class, completing a project, or getting your first business client.

If you work for a company, you can easily determine the price of your time by your salary. Stop working on little things and start focusing on bigger goals, where your time can be better used for something more productive, getting you closer to living your dream lifestyle. Do the following to help you manage your time and accomplish more in real time:

- Give time to everything that is important to you. This means setting aside time for people and tasks that add value.
- Prioritize your day based on completing the most important task that supports the goal you're working to achieve. You'll feel more in control when you're focused.
- Have time allocated to review and respond to daily and habitual distractions. Don't spend all day managing your in-box, voice messages, and social media posts.
- Take notes about your thoughts and ideas. Most things do not require your complete attention in the moment. Write your thoughts and ideas down so you can review them later and prioritize them based on existing goals.
- Set aside time for rest and relaxation. Make sure you have time set aside to read a book, self-reflect, and sleep.

 Action

> Identify one goal you want to complete by the end of the week. Invest one hour each day into completing that goal. And repeat.

HAVING BETTER CONVERSATIONS

What type of conversations are you having?

I enjoy good conversations. They add to the quality of my life. But I've also become more aware of the conversations I have and the people I have them with. As a result of increasing my awareness, I noticed which conversations were unproductive—ones in which I talked about things that I had no control over, such as what a friend was doing with his or her life. I was preoccupying myself with conversations about others to make sure I never had time, giving me an excuse that I had no control over my situation. I had all the solutions for that person's situation, but I didn't have solutions for my own life. Be mindful of these conversations—your 15 minutes is far too valuable to spend on them, and might be better spent reading a blog post on how to achieve your goals. Have better conversations by doing the following:

- Start conversations with people you admire, who live the life you want to live.
- Excuse yourself from discussions that are negative and don't add value.
- Ask yourself, how is this conversation contributing to my productivity and well-being?

During the Road to Financial Wellness tour, a woman from Boston stated that she had begun transferring $20 a month per paycheck into a savings account. At the time she wasn't quite sure if that was enough. Her coworkers and friends told her it would be better to put off saving until she could save more than $20. She added that after a year she had saved over $1,000, and that those same people who'd told her she needed to wait to save were now telling her what to do with her $1,000.

Who do you talk to about your finances?

The people around you can influence your financial well-being. There will be people who will offer advice on what you should or shouldn't do with your money. You may be spending money to keep up with their lifestyles. You may be thrust into a conversation about what so-and-so should do with his money, while at the same time wondering what to do with your own finances. Keep the following in mind:

- Be mindful about the people with whom you have conversations regarding your finances. This includes knowing the source of their information. If you're having these conversations, it's also good to know who the person is and how she is applying her advice in her own life.

- Take advice from individuals who are living the life you want to live and experts who understand your values and vision.
- Ask yourself, should I listen to investment advice from a friend who doesn't invest?

How comfortable are you with sharing your financial story with others?

The truth is that we're having these money conversations already. We learn our financial habits from our family, friends, coworkers, and through marketing messages. We make nonverbal statements about our financial capability by the clothes we wear, the cars we drive, and the houses we own. Some of these things just offer the illusion of wealth.

When you're aware of these nonverbal conversations, you aren't easily influenced. You accept that each person's financial situation and priorities are different from yours. You acknowledge what other people have, but your time and energy are focused on achieving dreams that are aligned with your values.

 Action

> Speak with a financial advisor or reach out to someone you admire and have a 15-minute conversation about money and life. It may change your perspective.

IMPROVING FINANCIAL RELATIONSHIPS

For a period of two months I worked for a finance company that targeted low-income urban residents. My former employer would send letters to people that stated that they were preapproved for loans. The letter looked like a check and said that all that the recipient needed to do was to give us a call, and we'd process the paperwork. My job was to get as many loans booked as possible, and I was incentivized to close as many as I could.

I didn't last long in the job. I couldn't come to terms with profiteering from people's lack of financial knowledge. Some of them were people with excellent credit scores who borrowed money through personal loans with interest rates that neared 30 percent. When we don't know about our financial options we're easy targets for companies that don't have our best interests in mind.

I used to blame creditors for my credit situation. My interest rates would go up and I'd be angry, but I would stay with the company. My bank and credit union would start charging annual fees for debit card usage and monthly fees for checking accounts and paper statements and I'd be annoyed, but I would stay with them. My car insurance premiums would go up regardless of my spotless driving record and I'd complain and argue, but I'd stay with that insurance company. I accepted these changes as out of my control. I believed it was the price I had to pay in order to get the services I needed. But as I increased my awareness, I began to know better. I don't mind paying for services, as long as I'm getting the kind of services I expect in return.

All financial services companies are in the business to make a profit, but not all financial institutions operate the same way. There are good and bad companies. Understand the missions of your financial institutions and know their terms and conditions.

Financial institutions, lenders, insurance providers, and other financial services organizations often change their terms of service, rates, and fees. They are required to inform you of these changes, but how many of us actually take the time to read the fine print on those notices?

You have limited or no control over how a financial institution conducts its business, but *you do have control* over whether or not you choose to work with them. Financial institutions remain in business because you give them *your* business.

Find the financial relationship that shares your money philosophy and vision. Many companies have vision statements—bold statements of what they aspire to be as organizations. Determine whether you agree with a company's vision and if it aligns with what you value.

There are many financial services organizations that do put people over profits, and there are many whose interest rates and fees are more favorable. You're only stuck in a financial relationship if you choose not to do anything about it. Have more control over your financial relationships by doing the following:

- Be proactive and start conversations with your financial institutions about their products and services.
- Be mindful of how you're being treated by your bank, credit card providers, and other financial services organizations. Don't let them dictate *your* rules.
- Know your values and what's important to you. Be prepared to leave when a financial institution's priorities and values do not align with yours.
- Know how your financial relationships are changing. If you've outgrown a financial relationship, it's time to move on and find one that's more reflective of your values.

 Action

Take control and review all your relationships with your financial institutions. Get to know their values, interest rates and fees, and products and services they offer. Then answer the following questions: Is this a company you trust and value? Is it providing the level of service you want?

In the next chapter we'll go over rules to help you gain control over spending. You'll learn how to spend mindfully, in order to prioritize the things you love over the things you like.

CHAPTER 10

Spending Rules

As you grow in awareness, you'll begin to ask yourself some interesting questions that get to the core of your values. I found myself doing exactly that a few years ago when I questioned the reasoning behind the things I bought. Why did I need to own two cars, live in an expensive apartment, and wear brand-name clothes? Why did I need the latest gadget and feel compelled to upgrade my phone every two years? And why did I pay for a monthly gym membership when I had access to a gym at work?

Asking these types of questions increased my awareness of my spending habits. I was making good money, but I was also spending most of it. Through asking myself these questions, I recognized that something was missing in my life—and that I was trying to fill it with things such as an $1,800 Movado watch and fancy weekend dinners with friends. I became aware that my mindless spending came from not knowing who I was, what I loved, and what I was working toward.

We often make purchase decisions without paying much attention to the thoughts and emotions that run through our mind. We're spending because of habit or responding to advertising and marketing messages. You may even spend to feel in control. But you're not in control when you're spending mindlessly. You might be purchasing goods that keep you from buying the things that you really love.

On my road trip and throughout this book I've shared my spending rules when discussing spending behaviors and habits. When you've grown in awareness, have gotten clear about your values, and have a vision for your life, you might find that having spending rules can help you make better purchasing decisions.

As you read this chapter, I want you to keep the following spending rules in mind:

- Spend less than you earn.
- Pay less for every purchase.
- Buy what you love, not what you like.
- Use credit for purposeful purchases.

It's now time to discuss how you can spend mindfully, afford more of the things you love, and use credit purposefully.

SPENDING MINDFULLY

You work to make money to spend, and I'm not asking you to stop spending—just to become more aware of how you spend your money and what you spend it on. If you are unhappy, it may be not because you spend the money you make, but rather because you spend more than you should and spend money on things that don't matter to you. You might spend money on expensive dinners and then wonder how you can afford to go on vacation. Or you might own a luxury car and also complain that you don't make enough money to save for a down payment on a home.

Spending mindfully is bringing increased attention to your thoughts and awareness of the present moment when making purchasing or financial decisions. When you are spending mindfully, you're making purchases based on conscious decisions, not spending habits. Have a plan for the money you make. I've found that some people spend money simply because they do not have a plan for the extra cash they've earned. When you spend mindfully, you're in control of how you're spending your money and your time. This gives you more control over your life.

SPEND LESS THAN YOU EARN

You *must* spend less than you earn. You'll need to cut your spending, and you can do this by examining your daily routines and eliminating things that cost money. If you realize that you no longer need a service, cancel it. In order to reach your financial goals you have to save some of the money you make. If you're mindlessly spending your entire income, you've placed your future well-being on the line.

PAY LESS FOR EVERY PURCHASE

When you spend mindfully, you'll choose to pay less for everything—from buying items only on sale or at a discount to using coupons to eliminating high-interest debt to lowering every other expense. Mindful spending means buying items you use regularly in bulk to save money. It also means paying less on the services you use—for example, lowering fees on cellphone carriers, cable subscriptions, and banking services. Review all your monthly expenses and bills and negotiate with the provider or lender for better rates and lower fees. If you determine that you can find a cheaper alternative, make the switch.

Cutting expenses has more power than increasing income. Reducing expenses has the dual effect of lowering your required monthly payments and lowering the amount you need for living expenses in the future.

Through the years I have used a system of questioning purchases that has kept me aware of how I am using my money. This tactic also creates a delay before the purchase is actually made that oftentimes has led me to just walk away. When you're determined to make a purchase for a number of reasons, stay mindful of how the money spent is impacting the quality of your life. Is the improvement temporary or long lasting? A purchase made today could impact your ability to retire early.

There are many ways to spend. We can go to the store, shop online, or use our mobile phones. It's so easy to shop that we often don't question the purchases we make—we only inquire about how soon we can get those purchases into our hands. When you're out shopping and you get the urge to buy something you hadn't planned on, ask yourself these three questions sequentially to maintain control:

1. Do I need it?
2. Do I need it now?
3. What will happen if I don't have it?

Asking these questions creates a delay and allows your brain to thoughtfully assess if the purchase is a rational one. I've used these questions often. It has even gotten to the point that when I am at a store and I see something I want but don't feel like asking myself these questions, I'll just walk away—because I know that it was obviously a purchase that I didn't need to make.

 Action

Use a debit card attached to a checking account that you set up specifically for variable expenses.

SPEND ON LOVES, NOT LIKES

Things you *love* will support your vision for your life. Things you *like* will distract you from achieving financial goals. When you practice financial awareness, you'll spend more on what you love and less on what you like.

You may have heard the acronym WANELO, which stands for *want, need, love*. I use this acronym to help me prioritize what I spend my money on. I've talked about the differences between needs and wants, but applying WANELO places the highest priority on things you love.

For example, let's take all the $40 dinners I once had in a span of 30 days. That's a total of $1,200—enough for an all-inclusive trip to the Dominican Republic for two people, with airfare included. I remember telling friends how much I needed to go on vacation and in the same breath complaining that I didn't have the money. But here I was, continuing to spend my money on things I liked in lieu of something I said I loved: traveling.

Over the past few years I have become more aware of the spending priorities of WANELO. I took that experience and followed my own priority list. If I don't absolutely love something, then I go down this priority list to determine if I need, want, or like it.

Love > Need > Want > Like

I've found that adding *love* and *like* to the spending-priority equation makes it easier to differentiate between *need* and *want*.

Why does *love* go before *need*? There are many things we need, and there may be even more things we want. But there are only a few things that we really love. When you spend on what you love, you're mindfully spending. Mindful spending is purposeful and adds value to your life.

For example, you may need a car but want a luxury vehicle. Using the spending priority just stated, you're aware that your dream car is a BMW. If owning a BMW is something you'll love, then no one should deprive you of ownership. If you truly love the car, then you'll make the necessary reductions in your expenses, find ways to increase your income, and sacrifice in other areas of your budget to make it happen. However, you might come to realize that spending $50,000 on a car—although affordable based on your finances—isn't worth the price tag because it doesn't pass the spending-priority equation as something you love.

Why is *want* before *like* in the spending-priority equation? There may be many things you like but you may not necessarily want them. To best explain this, let's use a common purchase that we all make at one point: a new smartphone. You may like Samsung phones but want an iPhone. You want the iPhone, but if you're worried about the cost, you must determine whether only the iPhone will meet your needs or if the Samsung can instead. However, if you've come to love the iPhone because it adds value in your life, then you're making the most mindful purchase by getting it.

Take a moment and reflect. Ask yourself this question: How many purchases have I made that I really love?

Financial awareness—including knowing what you love and what you're willing to pay—helps you prioritize making purchases that won't derail you from reaching your financial goals. Spending on things you love will bring happiness because those purchases add value in your life.

Action

Look around your home and find one object you bought recently that you absolutely love. What thoughts or feelings come to mind?

USE CREDIT PURPOSEFULLY

As I've traveled around the world I've come to realize how credit can empower people to build purposeful lives. Access to credit has provided the necessary means for people to build businesses to earn income and improve the quality of their lives. As a citizen of the United States, for example, I was able to afford college because of student loans. A college education helped me to get a job, and I was able to get to work because I financed a car. Credit is a financial tool that can allow us to move up the economic ladder. But mindless use of credit can also lead us into the pit of financial despair.

Wealth is a result of financial control. Debt results from the uncontrolled use of other people's money.

Credit can have a positive or negative impact on your lifestyle. Be mindful of how you use credit and keep track of your credit use. This can be done by monitoring your credit score and reviewing your credit reports annually. A strong and healthy credit history can mean access to credit with better terms and conditions. This can enable you to finance a much-needed car, own your dream home, and further your education. An excellent credit history can help you to get financing for business ventures and opportunities that can generate income or increase assets. An excellent credit history can also help you to eliminate debt by giving you access to refinancing and consolidation loans.

Credit should be used with a purpose. That purpose should be to improve your capability for earning a higher income. For instance, if you finance a car that enables you to go to work and earn a paycheck, or buy a home in a better neighborhood with a better school system for your children, or pay for college or trade school to get a new job or land a promotion, the credit you use is for a purpose other than just consuming.

However, keep in mind that when you're shopping for a new car or a house and the lender approves you for a specific loan amount, this does not mean it's an amount you can afford. The lender is not factoring in your lifestyle choices or your vision for your life. The lender is only looking at a bunch of numbers and a set of information that represents only a fraction of who you are. When you're aware of your vision and values, you won't let someone else tell you how much you can spend. Credit can be used purposefully to help us achieve goals and reach milestones.

Be mindful about using credit to positively impact your well-being long-term. It should rarely be used to pay for living expenses or consumption of goods that don't provide any return. When you use credit for a purpose, you'll find faster ways to repay the debt. When credit is used for mindless consumption, it gets more difficult to repay as time goes on. Ask yourself, how does this loan improve my life in the long term?

Take control of your credit use by being mindful of the following:

- Purchase on credit only if you're buying long-lasting assets with short-term financing.
- Don't finance items for a period longer than their usable lives.
- Think of the interest on a loan as an investment and determine the return on that investment.

 Action

After pulling your credit report from AnnualCreditReport.com, review your outstanding loans and write down the purpose for each open credit line you hold.

You have more control than you think when it comes to spending money. When you're aware of your values, you can develop better spending habits that help you achieve financial goals and support your vision. In the next and final chapter, I'll teach you how to live mindfully and take control to create a purposeful life.

CHAPTER 11

Living Mindfully

Imagine reaching your destination but not remembering the journey. When you are living mindfully, you're fully aware of what is going on around you and of everything that you do.

When you're living mindlessly, it means that you may be living your life based on other people's values and making choices that do not support your well-being. Living mindlessly is a life on autopilot, in which you're not in control of your own actions. It's a state of living in which you're doing things just to keep busy.

Living mindfully means you're present and aware, and making decisions that improve your current lifestyle. You're in control of your actions. You're able to achieve financial goals and progress toward your vision for your life. At the same time, you're able to enjoy life as it happens.

There are many things in life we cannot control, but the one thing we do have control over is our thoughts. Self-awareness increases your ability to recognize thoughts that are either destructive or supportive. Living mindfully is addressing negative thoughts and curtailing them, while allowing positive thoughts to control your actions. These *mindful* actions help you progress toward living your dream lifestyle.

Take control of your life by practicing mindfulness and doing the following:

- **Be deliberate with your thinking.** Even with clear values and a vision for your life, your environment can still impact your thoughts; give attention to thoughts that improve your situation.

- **Seek to understand, not react to, a situation.** Many things will happen that are out of your control, but how you react is up to you. Your initial reaction may be based on an unhealthy mindset, so give yourself time to understand your feelings and thoughts.

- **Remain present in the moment by observing, listening, and engaging.** You don't need to have a reaction or a response to every situation. Think about how the information or situation applies to your current life. Ask questions that can help you clarify how the information or situation impacts your future.

- **Give time to things that matter.** Stop checking your social media networks, text messages, and e-mail whenever you're bored. Instead, use the time to complete a task that contributes to your happiness, such as reading a book, learning a new skill, or calling a loved one.

Living mindfully means awareness that today is as good as any day to create your path to early retirement, to change your relationship with your employer, and to have new experiences. Living mindfully means you're aware of how money impacts your relationships, and the value of investing and insurance to secure and protect the life you're creating.

BUILDING YOUR FREEDOM FUND

When you're living mindfully, you're aware of the decisions you make daily that can help you achieve retirement sooner. You're saving more than you spend and controlling lifestyle inflation. You are purposeful in your saving to gain your freedom to pursue work that matters to you.

Imagine, for instance, that your cost of living is $35,000 per year and that you've saved $350,000: You've given yourself 10 years in which you won't have to work. Imagine what you could do or the things you could pursue within that time frame.

Have you ever wished you could take a six-month break from work?

Start a freedom fund. Similar to an emergency fund, a freedom fund is focused on saving enough money to cover your living expenses. However, the purpose is quite different: Instead of planning for an emergency, you're planning for a lifestyle change.

For example, let's say your income is $4,000 per month and you currently spend $2,000 per month on living expenses. If you saved half your income for one month, you would buy yourself one month of freedom. If you continue to save half your monthly income for an entire year and kept your lifestyle at the same reduced level, you could save $24,000, giving you an entire year of freedom.

Think about your living expenses and your current income. If you're living below your means, you're able to save much of your income to pay for living expenses in future months. Conversely, if you're living above or at your means, it gets much tougher to buy your freedom.

There are three things that you can do today to help you lower your living expenses and contribute toward your freedom fund: Cut expenses, save money on all purchases, and stop spending.

It's easier to reduce expenses than it is to earn more money. Again, reducing expenses has the dual effect of lowering your required monthly payments and lowering the amount you'll need in the future for living expenses.

When you cut expenses, you're finding more money without exchanging more of your time for it. This is the best way of increasing your monthly cash flow. Look at your budget to identify areas where you can reduce expenses.

All the small purchases and expenses may fall through the cracks, which can derail your efforts. However, don't forget about the big items you've financed, such as your car, home, or college education. You can find substantial savings by refinancing or finding the cash to pay big-ticket items off. To help you determine what expenses can be reduced or eliminated, answer the following:

■ Do you need cable or any of the other subscription services that you're paying for but not using?

- Can you reduce the interest rates on your loans and credit cards, thus reducing your payments?
- Are you able to negotiate with your landlord to pay less rent, or can you refinance your home mortgage?

Save where you can and decrease the amount you pay for things you need and want.

Consider using coupons and shopping for items only when they are on sale. Negotiate with each and every company that you pay to get a lower rate. You'll be surprised at the lengths some companies will go to in order to keep your business. If a company won't make a change in your favor, find an alternate provider.

I've already talked at length in previous chapters about spending. Remember, mindless spending can impact your ability to save, get out of debt, and leave an unsatisfying job. Be more mindful of how you're spending and cut unnecessary expenses to build up your freedom fund. There are certain purchases you don't need to make. When you're living mindfully, you'll reduce spending to support your road to financial wellness.

 Action

Start your freedom fund. Since you know how much you spend each month, take control and contribute to a fund that will allow you to take time off to explore your interests.

DON'T QUIT YOUR JOB

We place a big emphasis on the 40-hour workweek when we don't have a vision for our lives. We continue to define ourselves by our salaries and titles because we aren't clear about our values and our self-worth.

You are more than your salary and your job title. When living mindfully, you're aware of your love, needs, wants, and likes and the resources needed to live a purposeful life.

Do you want to quit your job?

I'm asked by many people about the necessity of quitting their jobs to find their purpose in life. Many individuals anguish over the decision to leave the stability of a job for the unknown. However, when you're living mindfully you understand that a job is the instrument that gives you financial means, enabling you to live your dreams.

I left my job, but I was also set up financially to take a couple of years off from working a traditional job. There's an allure to quitting a job and finding your purpose in life—but trust me, it's difficult to find your purpose or work on your interests when you're struggling to pay for basic living expenses. You don't need to quit your job to gain control over your life. It is much easier to have a source of income when you are figuring out the steps you need to take to live your purpose.

Change how you think about your job.

For the most part, your job isn't what's keeping you from living your dream lifestyle; how you're spending and saving money is. You can keep your job, but you need to change your mindset about it.

When you have a vision for your life, it's much easier to think of work purely as the source of income that helps you achieve your vision. When you have a vision for your life, you spend less time on complaining and more time on planning to achieve your goals. This allows you to mentally detach from the monotony and bureaucracy of your job, but still remain engaged in the work that you do.

Your job, as a source of money, can help you to pay off debts and build that freedom fund, so it's important to remain effective and contribute 100 percent at the workplace.

You might dislike aspects of your job, but it's something you're getting paid to do. Stick with the job until you've positioned yourself to have an improved financial situation. This improved situation could mean that you have other sources of income, that you've reduced your expenses, that you're out of debt, that you've built up your emergency fund, that you have a freedom fund, or all of the above.

Mindfully plan your career move.

If you're still unhappy with your job, take the steps necessary to eliminate the need to keep a job you dislike. Stop the mindless spending, downsize the lifestyle, and cut expenses until you can achieve some financial goals that bring you closer to your dream job.

If you determine that you can't quit right now, try to make your time spent at work more valuable. Your job could be offering opportunities to gain new experiences. Invest your time in being part of new projects, and attend workshops and training programs to learn new skills. These are opportunities to learn something new and add skill sets that may change the way you work and improve the way you think about your job.

Network with other employees in different parts of your company by participating in community events and company-wide meetings. Gaining new experiences and skills, and having an expanded network, can be useful in getting a promotion, moving to a new department, or helping you get a higher-paying job with another company.

Increase your take-home pay and take advantage of company benefits.

Improve your work life by staying on top of your income and reviewing your pay stubs frequently for changes that may need to be addressed or made. For example, perhaps you should change the number of dependents you've declared or increase your 401(k) plan contributions to decrease taxes. Find out if your employer offers classes and training programs. Inquire about tuition reimbursement and enroll in courses that make you more valuable. Get to know all the benefits offered to you, because you might be missing out on free money, opportunities to increase your income, or both.

In my previous job my employer offered an employee stock purchase program. I was able to buy company stock at a reduced market price and use paycheck deductions for the purchase. The company also offered money for attending programs aimed at improving employees' well-being, such as finance workshops, online courses, and gym memberships. In addition, my company offered a tuition reimbursement program that I used to pay for my MBA. And almost a year after graduating with my master's degree, I was offered an executive-level position across the country.

The larger your network and the more skills and experiences that you have, the easier it may be to find the right job and the right company. Before quitting your job, make every attempt to use your income and benefits to set yourself up for success in the future.

Action

Call your human resources manager and ask about available training and tuition reimbursement.

TRAVELING THE WORLD

Do you want to find your purpose?

I had to travel out of the country to define my purpose and gain clarity about my vision for my life. But traveling out of the country *isn't necessary*. What I've learned is that traveling takes us away from the familiar. We see different things and are exposed to new experiences. We meet new people and have different conversations. This provides a new kind of perspective that allows us to think differently about our situations.

When you're in the thick of things, it's hard to see much of anything else. If you're having the same type of conversations, doing the same type of job, or taking the same road to and from work, you're not gaining any new data or information. You need to gain new experiences and meet new people to change your perspective.

Plan for new experiences. Don't just look to escape your life when planning your trip. Purposefully plan your trip to improve your overall well-being. You'll find that this can be done at any point in time and accomplished closer to home.

Expand your inner circle of friends. Grow your network and engage with people who share your values and interests. You'll have new conversations and become exposed to new ways of thinking that can impact how you view your life.

You can do the following to break up your routine and have new experiences and conversations:

- Join groups that provide you with the opportunity to meet people you want to associate with.
- Participate in clubs that do the things you're interested in.
- Find a weekend when you can make your way to the nearest city you've wanted to explore. Exploring a new city provides many opportunities to have new conversations and gain new experiences that could change your perspective.

Do you want to travel the world?

You don't need to travel the world to find your purpose. However, it certainly can help. You also don't need a lot of money to travel. But you do need to plan accordingly and set financial goals that correspond with traveling the world. Understand the financial situation that's requiring you to work. What bills or expenses do you have? How much money do you have saved? What do you hope to accomplish during your travels? What do you envision doing after you've stopped traveling?

 Action

Join a local or community group focused on one of your interests. Get involved, meet new people, and have new conversations.

LENDING MONEY TO FAMILY AND FRIENDS

Part of living mindfully is understanding your family dynamics and how money plays a role in your relationships.

As you continue your journey on the road to financial wellness, you'll have times when people will ask you for money. They might be facing tough financial situations, and you might be their *only* salvation.

During a period of unemployment I asked my mother and some of my friends to lend me money to make my car payments. Because of the relationship I had with them, they helped me out. But when they asked for their money back, I was in disbelief that they couldn't understand my financial struggles.

When my finances improved, various family members and friends asked me for money to help with making a mortgage payment, putting food on the table, paying business expenses, or covering a car payment. If I had the money I lent it to them, with the expectation that it would be returned. But I should have remembered my own experience.

When we are in a tough financial situation, we aren't planning a way to get out of our predicament—we're just thinking about doing whatever needs to be done to pay for what's due. We're aware of what's happening, but not mindful of our options to improve our future well-being. During that time in my life, I certainly wasn't doing all I could to change my situation.

Although my family and friends helped me during a tough time, they also enabled me to continue with my bad financial habits. Having a loved one lend money can be the much-needed lifesaver that can alter the course of your life in a positive way. But without awareness of the root of your actual problem and a lack of a plan, you'll find yourself back in the same situation, blaming your family and friends if they are unable to help you in your time of need.

I have borrowed money from and lent money to family and friends. I have been on both sides of the fence. Neither side left me with a good feeling. As my finances have improved, I have developed this philosophy: *Don't lend money to anyone.*

My philosophy doesn't mean that I never give money to someone who needs it, but the big difference is my awareness of the financial impact that giving money can have on my well-being. If I have money to lend, I will help. But before I do, I determine if the money I lend is money I can live without and will not need. If I calculate that it will hurt my financial situation, I follow my money philosophy and don't lend the money, and I can say no without guilt. If I can lend money, I do so as a way to pay it forward. That way, the money I give is always repaid.

 Action

List the instances in which you've borrowed or lent money to family and friends. Then answer the question, "What were the outcomes of this money exchange?" Afterward, create your own money philosophy on lending to family and friends.

MAKING MONEY WITH MONEY: INVESTING

We live in a society in which the size of our salary is an indicator of success. The harder you work, the better your job, the larger your salary, the higher your quality of life. However, the key to early retirement and regaining control over your time is not exchanging more of your time for money but making money from money. Investing your money enables you to earn money with money. There is risk involved, but with mindful investing and planning, you'll have your money working for you.

With investing, you can be tempted by instant gratification. For example, you may have heard a hot stock tip or some buzz over a new tech stock that's about to go public. If you make an investment based on hearsay, you're not making a mindful decision. In many ways you will have gone back to mindless spending—on stocks, in this case— that lacks guidelines to ensure that the risk of losing your money is reduced.

During the Great Recession, many people were telling me to buy as many bank stocks as I could because they were on sale. As the stock prices continued to drop, I stuck with my investment philosophy: Buy stock at the lowest price I can once the price starts to climb back up. Unfortunately, one of my family members bought thousands of dollars' worth of Washington Mutual stock, believing some of the hype. The next day, the bank declared bankruptcy, and its assets were sold. She lost everything.

The lesson I learned about investing during the recession was simple: I should be as purposeful with buying stocks as I am with any other purchase I make.

Investing is an opportunity that can bring peace of mind today.

Think of investing as an opportunity to take care of yourself right now, not just at retirement in your 70s. The sooner you start investing, the more time your contributions will have to grow. You're using the power of time to your benefit to increase your money in the future.

You don't have to start investing in the stock market directly. Begin by contributing to your employer-sponsored retirement plan— frequently it's a 401(k). If your employer matches a portion of your contributions, make sure you contribute at least the minimum amount to get the employer match. *An employer match is like getting free money for investing money.* If you do not take advantage of employer matching, you're leaving money on the table.

Additionally, you can open up a brokerage account and start investing in index funds and trading stocks and bonds. Before investing, you must grow your knowledge about investing basics and be mindful of the reasons you're investing. How does investing contribute to your financial wellness? Are you investing for short-term gains or long-term success?

Take the time to research new companies that enable you to buy single shares of stocks. This is a good way to understand how the market works without risking too much of your cash assets.

 Action

Speak to a financial advisor or your defined contribution plan administrator about your 401(k) investment options.

PROTECTING YOUR LEGACY: INSURANCE

The best time to buy insurance is *today*, not sometime in the future.

As you approach the end of this book, I wanted to make sure the topic of insurance was addressed. We've grown up with so much financial and world uncertainty that we should be able to appreciate that having life insurance protects your family and other loved ones in case the worst happens. Insurance products offered by companies can and do vary quite remarkably. There are so many nuances, terms and conditions, and fees that I recommend you speak with an expert to truly understand your insurance options.

Insurance plays a key role in protecting you or your family in the event of an economic loss. You may not be thinking of insurance, because you might still feel invincible. But I hope that you've learned that although there are many things you can control, you can't control when you die.

You don't need a lot of insurance. You need the right amount of insurance. When creating your plan, you'll want to speak with a financial expert who understands insurance—and the various types that are available—to help you determine the specific product and amount that you need.

Thinking about our inevitable demise is grim, but as I've said throughout the book, you only live once—and if you've done it right you can leave behind a legacy for your family and loved ones.

Action

Find out how much life insurance you have through your employer. Speak with a financial advisor and find out how much life insurance you actually need.

FINDING AN EXPERT

During the road trip I had a conversation with a young professional man who shared an experience he'd had with a financial expert. The young professional mentioned that he'd spent 60 hours on gathering documents, thinking about his future, and speaking with the financial advisor. The advisor helped him create a budget and an investment strategy. However, he was reluctant to take the advice from the advisor without consulting his brother.

"I wanted to make sure this plan made sense," he said.

"What profession is your brother in?" I asked.

"He's in information technology," he responded.

"What experience does he have with creating a budget or investments?" I countered.

There is absolutely nothing wrong with speaking with trusted sources to help you gain a better understanding of your situation. However, you need to be mindful of whom you're having these financial conversations with. A financial expert has been trained to help with financial situations, just as an information technology professional has been trained to deal with technology.

Why are you taking expert advice from a person who may not be an expert?

The more financially literate and aware you are of your finances and your values, goals, and vision for your life, the easier you'll find it to speak with experts and apply their knowledge to helping you achieve your dreams.

Ask family and friends about the financial experts they use. There are many types of experts—from money coaches to budget planners to licensed financial advisors. Set up meetings with different experts, but do not commit to anything until you've read and understood their recommendations. Choose planners who are fee based, rather than commission-based planners who derive their income from selling financial products. Know their stories and backgrounds. If applicable, check their licenses and certification status. And ask to speak with existing clients, or request testimonials.

Should you pay an expert for money advice or guidance?

My straightforward answer to this question is yes. I've wondered why some people are willing to pay hundreds of dollars on concert tickets or sign up for an annual gym membership but don't like the idea of paying for advice from a financial expert or a life coach or an app.

When you're living mindfully, you understand that there are people living the life you want to and that these are the people you want to learn from. You can find a mentor, an advisor, or a coach to help you reach your goals. You're mindfully spending when you're investing in tools—that is, paying fees to experts—that improve your future. You'll spend less time trying to understand money and more time implementing your plan to live your dream lifestyle in this lifetime.

 Action

Find a fee-only certified financial advisor and schedule your first consultation.

Conclusion

Congratulations. You've journeyed to the end of this road trip. You now have more knowledge of your thoughts and feelings, you've learned how to create a roadmap to reach your destination, and you've learned to set goals based on your values and your vision.

First, understand that practicing awareness is an ongoing exercise that you must integrate into your daily routine. Simply asking a series of whys—such as "Why are things the way they are?" or "Why was this decision made?"—will help you gain a better understanding of your mindset. As you work on cultivating a healthy money mindset, get clear about your values, define that vision for your life, and live with a money philosophy.

Then use the YOLO budget as your framework to create a spending plan that aligns your financial goals with your values. It is a living plan that can and should change as you progress toward your vision. Understand the importance of this budget framework to create the lifestyle you want and to reach the goals you've set.

And remember, you can take control by being proactive and responsive. Improve your conversations and financial relationships by engaging with people and organizations. I hope you'll take what you've learned and use the knowledge gained to navigate toward your destination on the road to financial wellness. Revisit sections of the book often to reinforce the lessons you've learned.

Finally, and most important, you only live once, so define what living once means to you and take control to create a life you'd want to read about. From this point on, your journey continues.

Now, let me ask you:

"How would you write your story?"

Index

Abundance mindset, 18–19, 20, 24, 27
Account aggregation services, 129
ACT process, 14. *See also* Awareness; Control; Planning
Action steps:
  bucket list, 126
  conversations, 134, 152
  credit, 58, 143
  debit card and variable expenses, 140
  dual checking accounts, 101
  expenses, 101
  financial advisors, 134, 155, 157
  financial institutions, 136
  financial knowledge, 127
  financial organization, 130
  financial principles, 40
  financial status, 58, 59, 60, 62
  freedom fund, 148
  goals and time management, 132
  life insurance, 156
  loves versus likes, 142
  money philosophy, 153
  relationship with money, 20
  retirement, 62
  saving, 45, 110
  spending, 22, 43, 48, 49, 52, 56
  training and tuition programs, 151
  use of time, 23, 56
  values, 35, 50
  vision for life, 38
AnnualCreditReport.com, 57, 58, 143
Assets:
  building, to generate income, 9, 20, 23, 82, 93–94, 104, 120, 142
  credit and, 115, 143
  emergency fund and, 88, 108
  liquid, 59
  net worth and, 58–59, 81–83, 93
  time as, 10, 23, 43, 54–55, 130
Automatic bill payments, 99, 100, 129
Automatic funds transfer:
  to checking account, 103–104, 105, 107, 128–129
  to savings account, 44, 45, 100
Available money, calculating and adjusting in budgets, 90, 92–93
Avalanche method, of debt reduction, 117–118
Awareness:
  importance of, 15–16, 159
  knowing about spending habits, 41–62
  knowing where you are starting, 17–29
  knowing where you want to go, 31–40
  purposeful life and increasing of, 126–127
  see also Self-awareness

Balance transfers, debt reduction and, 113, 115, 116
Banks. *See* Financial institutions
Bargain hunting, spending habits and, 51–52
Blogs and podcasts, learning from, 127
Borrowing. *See* Debt; Interest rates, on loans
Brand-loyalty spending, 49–50
Brokerage account, opening of, 154–155
Budgeting, 67–96
  budget as spending plan, 68, 72
  common reasons for avoiding, 71–72
  fear of lifestyle change and, 68–70
  fear of lifestyle change, ways to manage, 70–74
  frameworks for, 73–74
  purposes of, 68
  tools for, 72–73
  ways to stay motivated about, 96
  YOLO lifestyle and, 74–77
  see also Purposeful money strategy; YOLO budget

Cable subscription costs, reducing of, 139, 147
Cash, spending only, 95
Cash flow:
  budgeting and, 81–82
  calculating of, 59–60, 90, 92–93
  debt elimination and, 114
Clock time, 130
Club savings accounts, 103
Clutter, avoiding of, 128
Consolidation, of debt, 111–112, 113, 115, 116, 142

Consumption, illusion of control and, 123–124
Control:
  debt elimination and, 114–115
  of and by money, 19–20, 21
  spending and illusion of, 48–49, 123–124, 137–138
Control, taking of, 121–122, 159
  by creating purposeful life, 123–136
  by living mindfully, 145–157
  with spending rules, 137–143
Conversations, having better:
  about finances, 127, 133–134
  generally, 132, 151–152
Cost of living:
  financial education and, 13
  freedom fund and, 146–147
  vision for life and, 85
  see also Expenses
Credit:
  misuse of, 116
  reviewing credit reports regularly, 127, 129, 142
  using as financial tool, 53–54, 57
  using purposefully, 142–143
  see also Debt
Credit cards:
  balance transfers and debt reduction, 113, 115, 116
  electronic billing and, 128
  reducing fees of, 148
  spending and, 95
  see also Debt
Credit score:
  benefits of good, 142
  importance of knowing, 56–58
  unneeded credit and, 111
Credit unions. *See* Financial institutions

Debit cards:
    monitoring spending with,
        47–48
    spending convenience and, 140
    variable expenses and, 100,
        140
Debt:
    avoiding in future, 120
    consolidation of, 111–112,
        113, 115, 116, 142
    eliminating of high-interest,
        139
    minimum monthly payments
        and, 116–119
    money mindset and, 111,
        112–115
    net worth and, 58
    retail therapy and, 49
    root causes of and
        responsibility for, 114
    time value of money and, 55
    types of, 115
    use of time and, 22–23
    ways to eliminate, 73–74, 89,
        115–120
    YOLO and, 8, 10
    YOLO budget and, 89, 94
    see also Credit; Interest rates,
        on loans
Delayed gratification, saving and,
        104
Direct deposits, of pay, 99, 101,
        107, 129. *See also* Automatic
        funds transfer
Do Not Call registry, 129
Dreams:
    happiness as result of realized,
        24–25
    living own, 25–26
    vision for life and, 37–38
Dual checking accounts, 98–101
    benefits of, 99
    setting up of, 99–100

Electronic billing, 128–129
E-mail:
    financial organization and,
        128, 129
    managing time spent on, 146
Emergency fund, 26, 43
    allocating money to, 44, 88,
        93, 100, 103–108
    financial goals and, 86–87, 110
    living expenses for six months
        and, 59, 88, 105, 106–107,
        108
    net worth and, 82
Emotions:
    debt and, 112
    mindfulness and reactions to
        situations, 146
    money mindset and, 2, 18–19,
        20, 27
    purposeful life and, 126–127
    self-awareness and, 16, 20
    spending and, 21–22, 41,
        48–50
Employer, using benefit
        programs of, 13, 150, 154
Engagement, mindful living and,
        96, 146, 151
Equifax, 57
Evil, money and, 19
Exchange value of time:
    mindful living and, 153
    money mindset and, 10, 22–23,
        29, 55, 130
    retirement and, 61, 110
Expenses:
    budget frameworks and, 73–74
    calculating of cash flow and,
        60
    checking account for, 100
    having savings to cover six
        months of, 59, 88, 105,
        106–107, 108
    reducing of, 147–148

Expenses (*continued*)
  spending less than income
    and, 139–140
  tracking for budget creation,
    81–82
  see also Cost of living
Experian, 57
Experiences, purchase of things
    versus, 27, 34, 55, 126,
    151–152
Family, avoiding lending money
    to, 152–153
Fear, money mindset and, 19–20
Feelings. *See* Emotions
Fees, finding lower, 15, 139, 157
50-30-20 budgeting rule, 73
Finances, organizing of, 128–130
Financial advisor:
  finding and using, 134, 155,
    156–157
  investing and, 37
Financial awareness. *See*
  Awareness
Financial education:
  benefits of, 2, 12–13
  cost of ignorance and, 15–16
  importance of, 11–12, 13–14
  purposeful life and, 126–127
Financial freedom:
  defining in budget process, 77
  fund to ensure, 146–148
Financial guidelines, basic, 1
Financial institutions:
  amount of credit offered by,
    versus ability to pay, 143
  awareness and, 15
  brokerage accounts and, 154–155
  financial education and, 13, 14
  improving relationships with,
    134–136
  simplifying relationships with,
    128–129

  spending and, 95
  see also Insurance, importance of
Financial wellness, defined, 5
Fixed expenses:
  defined, 98–99
  dual checking accounts and,
    99–101
  tracking of, 91
401(k) plans, 13, 26, 87, 88, 97,
    110, 150, 154, 155
Freedom fund, building of,
    146–148
Friends, avoiding lending money
    to, 152–153

Goals:
  budget frameworks and, 74
  credit as financial tool and, 54
  lifestyle and budgeting, 85–89
  prioritizing of, 89
  purposeful savings and, 106–107
  qualities of, 86–87
  short-, mid-, and long-term, 88
  spending and, 21–22, 140–142
  time management and,
    131–132
  see also Values

Habit spending, 46–48
Happiness:
  money and, 19, 24–25,
    124–125
  purposeful life and, 124–126
  values and, 32, 36
Hope ("hearing other people's
    stories"), 2

Immediate savings, 108
Income:
  calculating and tracking for
    budget creation, 81–82,
    90–91

cash flow calculation and, 60
keeping job and, 148–151
spending less than, 139
using assets to increase, 9, 20, 23, 82, 93–94, 104, 120, 142
using bonuses for debt reduction, 116
see also Paychecks
Insurance:
importance of, 155–156
knowing rates of providers, 135
Interest rates, on loans:
credit score and, 57
negotiating for lower, 114–115, 116, 139, 148
paying attention to, 135
prioritizing when eliminating debt, 89, 117–118
Investing:
advantages of, 153–155
money as resource for, 77
in self, 23, 130
vision for life and, 37–38
YOLO and, 9–10
IRAs, 88, 110

Job, not quitting, 148–151

"Keeping up with Joneses," versus living own dreams, 25–26
"Know where you're starting," financial awareness and, 17–29
cultivating wealthy mindset, 23–29
relationship with money and, 19–20
scarcity and abundance and, 18–19, 20, 24, 27
spending and, 20–22
use of time and, 22–23

Knowledge. *See* Financial education

Late credit card payments, 116
Lenders. *See* Financial institutions
Lending money, avoiding of, 152–153
Liabilities, net worth and, 58. *See also* Debt; Expenses
Life insurance, importance of, 155–156
Lifestyle:
avoiding inflation of, 26
freedom fund and, 146–148
goals to improve, 87
see also Purposeful life, creating of
Liquid assets, net worth and, 59
Listening, mindful living and, 146
"Live fully but die broke," 121
"Living within your means," 82
Loans. *See* Debt; Interest rates, on loans
Long-term savings, 109
Lunch habits, spending and, 47–48
Mental accounting, versus budgeting, 65, 69
Mid-term savings, 109
Millennials, YOLO and, 7–8
Mindful living, 145–157
building freedom fund, 146–148
buying insurance, 155–156
cautions about lending to friends and family, 152–153
finding financial expert, 156–157
investing, 153–155
keeping job, 148–151
tips for, 146
traveling and, 151–152

Mindful spending, 138, 139
Mindless spending, 22, 46, 74
Minimum monthly payments, on
    debt, 116–119
Money:
    assessing relationship with,
        19–20
    methods of spending, 94–95
    using as tool, 19–20, 24–25,
        32, 76
Money mindset:
    budgeting fears and, 71–72
    as compass, 24
    consumption and values,
        123–124
    cultivating of "wealthy,"
        23–29
    debt elimination and, 111,
        112–115
    focusing on positive, 125
    impact of, 2–3, 17
    saving and, 43, 102–103
    spending and, 52–53
    time and, 10, 22–23, 29, 55,
        130
    vision and, 31
    YOLO budget, 89
    YOLO lifestyle, 8–10, 74–77
Money philosophy, 2–3
    about lending money,
        152–153
    budgeting and, 79
    debt elimination and, 114
    regarding credit, 113, 116
    relationship with financial
        institutions and, 135
    saving and, 104, 108
    vision for life and, 32,
        38–40
    YOLO budget and, 89

Needs versus wants, spending
    and, 52–53, 140–142

Negative discussions, avoiding
    of, 133
Negative net worth, 82–83
Negative thoughts, avoiding of,
    145
Net worth, calculating of, 58, 81,
    82–83, 93
Nonverbal statements, about
    financial status, 134
Notes, taking about thoughts and
    ideas, 132

Observation, mindful living
    and, 146
Online bill payment, 129
Online financial statements,
    advantages of, 128

Passport, electronic copy
    of, 128
Paychecks:
    automatic saving and,
        103–104, 107
    dual checking accounts and,
        99–100
    monitoring progress toward
        goals and, 107
    see also Income
Planning:
    building lifestyle budget and
        spending plan, 67–97
    importance of budgeting and,
        63–66
    improving credit and
        eliminating debt, 111–120
    using purposeful money
        strategy to spend and save,
        97–110
Positive net worth, 82–83
Purposeful life, creating of,
    123–136
    accumulating wealth and, 28
    by finding happiness, 123–124

by having better conversations,
127, 132–134
by improving financial
relationships, 134–136
by increasing awareness,
126–127
by managing time, 130–132
money mindset and, 3
by organizing finances,
128–130
society's values and
consumption, 123–124
values and, 33–34, 35–38
see also Mindful living
Purposeful money strategy,
97–110
dual checking accounts and,
98–101
saving and, 101–110

Real time, 130
Refinancing, of debt, 57, 93, 115,
142, 147–148
Rent, negotiating for lower, 148
Rest and relaxation, importance
of, 132
Retail therapy, spending habits
and, 48–49
Retirement planning:
budget frameworks and, 73–74
calculating of income versus
expenses in, 61–62
financial education and, 13
freedom fund and, 146–148
savings accounts and, 109–110
using employer-sponsored
program, 154
visions and, 37–38
Road to Financial Wellness tour,
5, 12, 32, 44, 133
Roth IRA, 110
Routines, spending and, 42–43,
68–69

Safety net. *See* Emergency fund
Saving:
automatic transfer of income
to, 44, 45, 100
budget frameworks and, 73–74
making habit of, 43–45
net worth and, 59
"paying self first" and, 28–29,
113
time and, 55
wealth and, 27–28
YOLO and, 8, 10
YOLO budget and, 88, 94
Saving, purposeful method for,
101–110
finding best financial
institution for, 102, 106
fund categories for, 108–110
having multiple accounts for,
103–105
implementing strategy for,
106–107
money mindset and, 102–103
preparing for, 105–106
Scarcity mindset, 18, 19–20, 24,
41, 76, 113
Self-awareness:
goals and, 89
mindful living and, 127, 145
money mindset and, 16, 24
spending and, 50, 84, 114
see also Awareness
Self-improvement:
purposeful life and, 126–127
use of time and, 23
Self-reflection, benefits of, 131
70-20-10 budgeting rule, 73
Short-term savings, 109
60 percent budgeting rule, 73
Snowball method, of debt
reduction, 118–120
Social Security card, storing
of, 128

Spending, 41–62
  analyzing of, 45–52
  awareness of role in life, 20–22
  bargain hunting and, 51–52
  brand-loyalty spending, 49–50
  calculating for budget creation,
    90, 91–92
  checking accounts for, 100–
    101
  financial analysis and, 56–62
  versus habit of saving, 27–28,
    43–45
  habit spending, 41–43, 46–48
  lack of vision and, 31
  mindful versus mindless, 22,
    46, 74, 138, 139
  money mindset and, 2
  needs versus wants and,
    52–53
  reducing for job flexibility,
    148–151
  retail therapy, 48–49
  versus saving, 27–28
  time's power and, 54–56
  tracking for budget creation,
    72–73, 79, 81–82
  values and, 33
  YOLO and, 9, 10
  YOLO budget and priorities,
    93–94
Spending, rules for, 137–143
  earnings and, 139
  loves, not likes and, 140–142
  mindfulness and, 138, 139
  paying less for purchases,
    139–140
  using credit purposefully,
    142–143
Stocks:
  brokerage accounts and,
    154–155
  mindfulness and purchase
    of, 154

taking advantage of employer's
    stock option programs, 13,
    150, 154
Stress, lessening with better
    financial decisions, 127
Student loans, 53, 57, 93, 142
  as fixed expense, 91
  paying off, 86, 87, 89, 115
  YOLO mindset and, 8
Subscriptions, reducing costs of,
    147

Tasks and chores, time
    management and, 131–132
Time:
  as asset, 10, 22–23, 43, 54–55,
    130
  determining price of, 132
  happiness and, 126
  lack of vision and disregard
    for, 31
  managing of, for purposeful
    life, 130–132
  mindful living and, 146
  money mindset and, 20
  using as resource, 54–56
Time value of money, 55
Training programs, for job
    improvement, 150
TransUnion, 57
Travel, benefits of and saving
    for, 151–152
Tuition reimbursement programs,
    150, 151

Unemployment. See Emergency
    fund

Values, 31–40
  aligning with happiness, 32,
    36, 124–125
  clarifying of, 32–35

credit and, 143
mindfulness and, 146
money philosophy and, 38–40
relationship with financial
    institutions and, 136
spending and, 9, 21
vision for life and, 35–38
see also Goals
Variable expenses:
available money and, 92,
    95, 96
defined, 99–101
dual checking accounts and,
    98–101, 103–104
tracking of, 91, 140
Vision, for life:
budgeting and, 80–85
credit and, 143
debt elimination and, 114
happiness and working
    toward, 125–126
mindfulness and, 146
relationship with financial
    institutions and, 135
values and, 35–38

WANELO. *See* Wants versus
    needs
Wants versus needs, spending
    and, 52–53, 140–142

Wealth:
goals to increase, 87
as result of financial
    control, 142
Wealthy money mindset,
    cultivating of, 23–29
avoiding lifestyle inflation, 26
happiness and, 24–25
paying self first, 28–29
pursuing own dreams,
    25–26
saving versus spending and,
    27–28
West, Mae, 7
Workcentric lifestyle, 35–36

YOLO (You Only Live Once):
lifestyle and, 74–77
millennials and, 7–8
mindset of, 8–10
YOLO budget, 93, 96, 159
debt elimination and, 113
exact number calculation for,
    90–93
financial goals and, 77–80,
    85–89
money allocation and, 93–95
vision of lifestyle and, 80–85
see also Budgeting; Purposeful
    money strategy